FORTS OF MARATHWADA

RUPESH MADKAR

Made with ♥ on the Notion Press Platform
www.notionpress.com

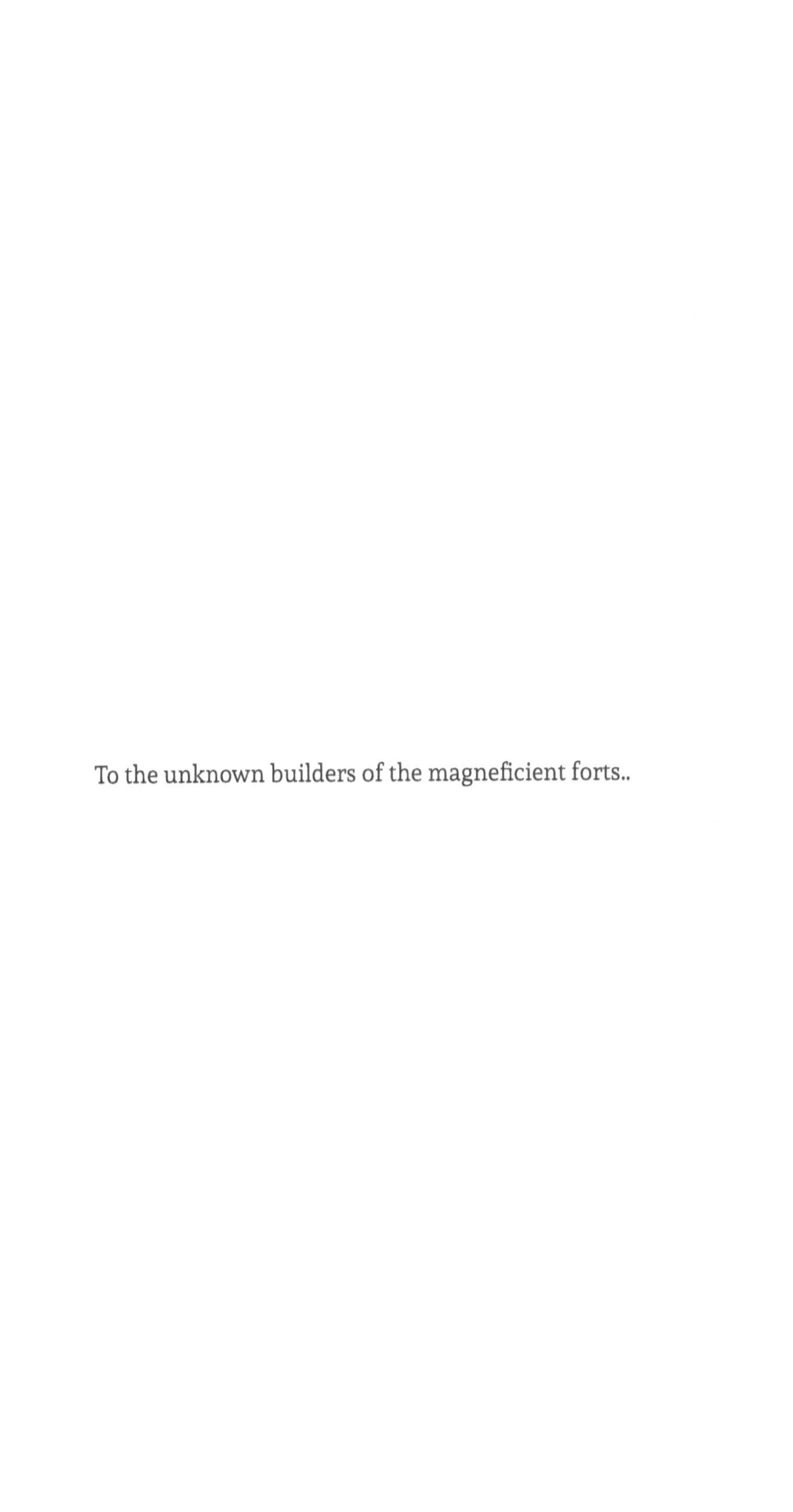

To the unknown builders of the magneficient forts..

Contents

Foreword   *vii*

Preface   *ix*

Acknowledgements   *xi*

   1. Forts: Meaning And Definition   1

   2. Types And Importance Of Forts   18

   3. Forts Of Marathwada: Hill Forts   41

   4. Forts Of Marathwada: Ground Forts   58

PYQ   79

FOREWORD

PREFACE

This year, starting from 2024, the New Education Policy (NEP) - 2020 was implemented for undergraduate courses in colleges, introducing a new curriculum. Within this, certain subjects were included under the title of Indian Knowledge Systems (IKS), one of which was a course titled "Forts of Marathwada." This subject was introduced in the first year of undergraduate studies for colleges under Dr. Babasaheb Ambedkar Marathwada University, Chhatrapati Sambhajinagar. Students from the Science, Commerce, and Arts streams enthusiastically opted for this course. Since it is related to the subject of history, I also began teaching it. However, I soon realized that my knowledge about the forts in Marathwada was rather limited. I had access to one or two books, but I realized that they were not affordable for students and were not comprehensive enough to cover the entire curriculum.

The available books are in Marathi, but there is no study material in English for students from Science and Commerce streams in English-medium colleges, which was another challenge. After teaching, I usually recommend some books for students to read, as is my habit. But in this case, I found myself wondering what I could suggest for students to read on this topic. Given that many undergraduate students in Marathwada have chosen this subject, this question felt pressing. I started gathering whatever resources I could find and began reading. I thought of writing or compiling a small book myself in both Marathi and English, tailored to the curriculum. However, I faced another challenge: finding a publisher. Today, with advances in technology, many self-publishing platforms are available. So, I decided to try this route and conduct this experiment.

In the course of writing this book, I did a lot of reading. I gained a wealth of knowledge about the many forts of Marathwada. Had I not taught this subject, or had this subject not been part of the curriculum, I probably wouldn't have read as much about the forts of Marathwada, let alone written about them. Driven by the question, "If there's nothing for students to read on this subject, what will they write in the exam?" I was able to compile, edit, and write this book. In this sense, just as teachers motivate students to read and study (or so I believe), students likewise motivate teachers to read, study, and write. This, too, is equally true.

Acknowledgements

Many people unknowingly contributed to the compilation, editing, and writing of this book. I received encouragement and support from Prof. Dr. Rohini Kulkarni-Pandhare, Principal of Government College of Arts and Science, Chhatrapati Sambhajinagar. All my senior colleagues at the college motivated me. Discussions with Dr. Ajaykumar Gandhi provided insights into self-publishing platforms. This book would not have been published without the valuable support of all these individuals, for which I am immensely grateful.

- Rupesh Madkar

I

Forts: Meaning and Definition

Index

1.1 Objectives

1.2 Introduction

1.3 Topic Discussion

1.3.1 What is a Fort

1.3.2 History of Fort Construction

1.3.3 Various Definitions of a Fort

1.3.4 General Characteristics of a Fort

1.4 Summary

1.5 Self-Study Questions

1.6 Books for Further Reading

1.1 Objectives

After studying this chapter, you will be able to:

- Understand what a fort is.

- Learn about the history of fort construction around the world.

- Understand the various definitions of a fort.

- Comprehend the general structure and form of a fort.

1.2 Introduction

Building forts has been considered an essential part of ruling throughout history. In monarchies or dictatorships, the king was regarded as the supreme authority, with all the wealth of the kingdom belonging to him. In many parts of the world, kings were viewed as "divine entities." Mentions of forts can be found in ancient times across many regions. Expanding one's territory and bringing as much land as possible under control was the primary goal of any king or ruler. This ambition led many rulers to adopt titles like "Chakravarti" (universal ruler) or "Prithvipati" (lord of the earth). In this pursuit, there arose a need for secure places for self-defense in the face of attacks. This need contributed to the development of the techniques for fort construction. In this chapter, we will explore what a fort is, the various definitions of forts, and the general characteristics of forts.

1.3 Topic Discussion

1.3.1 What is a Fort?

Rugged land, tough land, the land of rocks,
Gentle land, tender land, also a land of flowers, - Maharashtra Geet,
Govindagraj (original in Marathi)

Maharashtra is the land of forts. No other region in the world has as many forts as Maharashtra does. The forts constructed in the basalt rock of Maharashtra's terrain contributed to Govindagraj's poetic description of the land in the Maharashtra anthem. The network of forts in this region has deeply influenced the character of the people here. Major Graham, in his report on Kolhapur, said, "Each fort on a hilltop must have spoken to the people here, urging them to be self-reliant instead of depending on rulers, and instilling a sense of independence in the minds of even the smallest chieftains—this is a unique trait of the inhabitants of southern Maharashtra."

There are no rigid criteria for what exactly qualifies as a fort, but there are certain features or elements that are typically associated with it. According to the Marathi Encyclopedia, a fort is described as "a structure built for ease of defense against enemies and for maintaining control over the surrounding area." The term "durg" (fortress), derived from Sanskrit, was chosen to represent a fort in the Rajyavyavhar Kosh (State Administration Dictionary), commissioned by Shivaji Maharaj. The word "durg" essentially means an area that is difficult to penetrate or access. In the medieval era, the word "kila" (fort), derived from Arabic, was also adopted to refer to forts. This term has become more commonly used today.

In English, forts are referred to by terms such as castle, fort, citadel, and burg. In Marathi, terms like durg, giridurg (hill forts), dweepdurg (island forts), janjira, gadhi, kot, gad, balekilla (citadel) represent different types of forts. In short, a fort is a strong and fortified structure primarily designed for military defense, to protect against enemy attacks, and to safeguard the surrounding area. Throughout history, forts have held great importance as the key defensive posts of rulers, empires, and military forces. Forts are usually constructed from stone, bricks, wood, or mud, with strong walls, bastions, gates, and often defensive moats.

Forts can be square, circular, hexagonal, or even octagonal. In ancient India, for example, the Harappan civilization, settled along the Indus River Valley, had fortified towns, and excavations have revealed that Harappa itself was surrounded by a wall with a central citadel. During the Vedic and Brahmanic periods, cities were also fortified with walls and protected by surrounding moats. Kautilya's Arthashastra, a significant text on statecraft, also contains descriptions of fort construction, reflecting the architectural importance of forts.

The remnants found in the city of Pataliputra reveal that the city was fortified with a strong defensive wall and a moat structure. During the Gupta and Rashtrakuta periods, forts were not considered as crucial, yet they fortified their own palaces with strong defenses. In the pre-Islamic era, during the times of the Chalukyas, Shilaharas, and Yadavas, the importance of forts increased significantly. Most of the forts originate from this period, and although they may not be visible today, forts like Daulatabad (Devagiri), Salher-Mulher, Ankai-Tankai, Anjaneri, Markanda,

Rangana, Pavangad, Panhala, and Vishalgad are from the medieval period.

Salher Fort (Wikicommon)

1.3.2 History of Fort Construction

The tradition of fort construction appears to date back to ancient times. In the primitive era, humans felt the need for protection against wild animals and the elements, such as scorching sun, sever cold, and heavey rain. Initially, they relied on natural caves and rock shelters. Over time, early humans used available natural resources to create basic shelters, although their early efforts were focused only on temporary shelters. At this stage, humans were primarily nomadic, engaged in hunting and food gathering, and lived in groups. Temporary shelters were sufficient since they moved frequently.

As humans began practicing agriculture, they adopted a settled lifestyle, which demanded more permanent shelter. This led to the development of the earliest dwellings in the Indian subcontinent, with evidence of early homes found at Mehrgarh in present-day Pakistan. Later, in India and other countries, people began carving rock to create caves as shelter.

Mehergarh Ruins

The precise origins of fort construction are unknown. During the Egyptian civilization (3500–600 BCE), palaces were fortified with walls, bastions, and moats. In the Twelfth Dynasty (2000–1786 BCE), the fortress of Semna was built, establishing a tradition that continued over time. In Assyria (8th–7th centuries BCE), cities were surrounded by walls, with Khorsabad being a notable example. Babylon (1800–500 BCE) also fortified cities in this way. The Greeks had famous forts, such as the Tiryns citadel and the Acropolis in Athens.

In the Roman era, forts gained importance, and palaces resembled small, fortified castles. Many European forts were built in the Greco-Roman and Gothic architectural styles. Between 1000 and 1500 CE, the number of forts in Europe grew significantly, largely due to the Normans' influence, feudalism, and the Crusades. Famous forts from this era include Hedingham, Colchester, Pembroke, Deal, Kenilworth, Conway, Arundel, Dover, Edinburgh, and Windsor in England; Coucy-le-Château and Château de Chambord in France; Braunfels in Germany; Muiden in the Netherlands; Castel Sant'Angelo in Italy; Alcázar in Spain; Rumelihisarı in Turkey; Krak des Chevaliers in Syria; the Counts of Flanders castle in Belgium; and Kalmar in Sweden. Modifications continued, with improvements to fortresses such as Eilean Donan, Arundel, Blarney, Caernarfon, and Caerlaverock, as well as renovations to Renaissance-era castles like Maisons, Lafayette, Chenonceau, and Azay-le-Rideau.

Fort built in 11th century, Italy

Some forts were destroyed during World War I, yet remnants of many of these historic forts can still be seen today. The Kremlin in Russia serves as a prime example of a fortified citadel from this tradition.

Ancient Indian Literary References to Forts

Forts find mention in ancient Indian literature such as the Rigveda, Manusmriti, Arthashastra, Mahabharata (Shanti Parva), and various Puranas, where there is extensive discussion on the types of forts and their importance. In ancient India, the city of Mohenjodaro and other cities in the Harappa Civilization was fortified, with remnants indicating a citadel built in the center of the city. Many sites of the Harappan civilization reveal cities divided into two parts, with a fortified section, likely a citadel where influential figures lived, elevated from the lower part of the city. The citadel was separated from the lower city by fortifications, though sometimes the entire city was enclosed by walls.

Harappan Citadel (Wikicommon)

During the Vedic and Brahmanical periods, walls and moats were built around cities. The Rigveda uses the term "pur," meaning a settlement surrounded by protective walls. The Aitareya Brahmana mentions various forts, describing the three fires as protectors against the Asuras. In the Mauryan period, Kautilya's Arthashastra provides architectural descriptions, indicating a standardized approach to fort construction. After moving the Mauryan capital to Pataliputra, it seems the city was developed into a stronghold. Megasthenes' account describes Pataliputra as encircled by wooden fortifications with 64 gates and 500 bastions. Archeological remains suggest a surrounding moat and strong walls.

Although forts were less prominent during the Gupta, Vakataka, and Rashtrakuta periods, royal palaces and cities were often fortified. The 12th century saw the rise of hill forts under the Chalukya, Shilahara, and Yadava dynasties, marking a peak in fort construction in terms of quantity, even if their original forms are now lost. Forts like Devagiri (Daulatabad), Salher-Mulher, Ankai-Tankai, Anjaneri, Markanda, Trimbak, Rangna, Pavangad, Panhala, and Vishalgad are from this era.

During the medieval period, many forts were constructed, including notable examples such as the Red Fort in Delhi, Agra Fort, Ahmadnagar Fort, Bijapur Fort, and Bangalore Fort, all prime examples of ground forts. The Rajputs built prominent hill forts like those in Chittorgarh, Amber, Jodhpur, and Gwalior. In the 17th century, Shivaji Maharaj constructed numerous new forts in Maharashtra and renovated existing ones, equipping them with buildings, reservoirs, and defenses. Rajgad, Raigad, Purandar, Torna, Vishalgad, Panhala, Pratapgad, and sea forts like Sindhudurg, Vijaydurg, Jaigad, Khandeheri, Suvarnadurg, Arnala, Kulaba, Janjira, Padmadurg, were among these. In later periods, forts built by Shivaji were maintained, though European colonizers established new forts such as Fort William, Fort St. George, Fort St. David, and Aguada. Golconda, Trichinopoly, Penukonda, and Chandragiri forts also gained importance during this period.

In addition to the capital cities, local feudal lords constructed smaller forts known as gadhis, which were miniature replicas of larger forts. The architectural design of Indian forts shows influences from Norman fort structures as well as Saracenic architecture, which is particularly evident in Maharashtra's forts.

Agra Fort

Definitions of Fort

Various sources offer differing definitions of forts. In the Rigveda, the term 'pur' is mentioned, and the deity Indra is referred to as Purandara, meaning the "breaker of forts." Here, pur simply means a settlement surrounded by protective walls, as fortifications were not yet advanced. While terms like pur, durg, and kot appear in texts like the Amarakosha, the most fitting Sanskrit term for a fort is durgam, meaning "difficult to access."

The Marathi Vishwakosh defines a fort as a structure built to facilitate defense against enemies and control surrounding territories. Amarakosha describes it as "a fortified settlement located in an inaccessible place, such as a mountain." The English term "fort" originates from the French word fortis, meaning "strong." Thus, a fort is a structure designed to provide defense and control over surrounding areas.

In general, a fort is defined as a constructed area difficult to access. Another definition from dictionaries is "a place made safe with walls, moats, and other defenses." According to Kautilya's Arthashastra, a fort is a walled capital city that offers refuge to the king when besieged, allowing a prolonged fight against invaders.

In the Merriam-Webster dictionary, fort is defined as

"a strong or fortified place, especially : a fortified place occupied only by troops and surrounded with such works as a ditch, rampart, and parapet : fortification and a permanent army post"

General Structure of Forts

The structure and needs of forts vary by type, but certain features are common across fort types, giving them a general design. These elements include defensive walls, bastions, an outer wall, and a main entrance. The general structure of forts includes the following elements:

Fortification/ Fort Walls

Walls are strong stone constructions encircling the fort. It is not necessary to have walls on all sides; steep, impassable cliffs naturally protect certain sections. Some forts have only partial walls, connecting cliffs to secure the area. For instance, Tungi fort lacks walls but has a gate and bastions. In Maharashtra, some forts have chilkhati-style walls, where two walls are nested within each other, as seen at Raigad. The width of walls ranges from 3 to 10 meters, allowing a soldier to patrol with weapons. The walls of Vasai Fort, for instance, are wide enough to accommodate two cars.

Moats

A moat is a trench dug around the fort with a bridge over it, making attacks difficult. Moats often contained spikes and poisonous snakes. The moat around Chakan Fort was 30 feet deep and 15 feet wide, filled with water. Yashwantgad Fort has a 24-foot-wide and 13-foot-deep moat around most of its perimeter. Gopalgad Fort is surrounded by a 15-foot-deep moat on the south side, with seawater providing protection on the other sides.

Ravine

Beyond the moat, a raised area known as a ravine or glacis was built around the fort. The slope on the fort side of the ravine was designed so that if extended, the slope line would pass over the fort wall, making it difficult for attackers to fire from the other side. In the event of a siege, fort soldiers would station in the ravine, using small cannons and rifles. Attackers had to clear the ravine before advancing their artillery to target the fort walls and bastions.

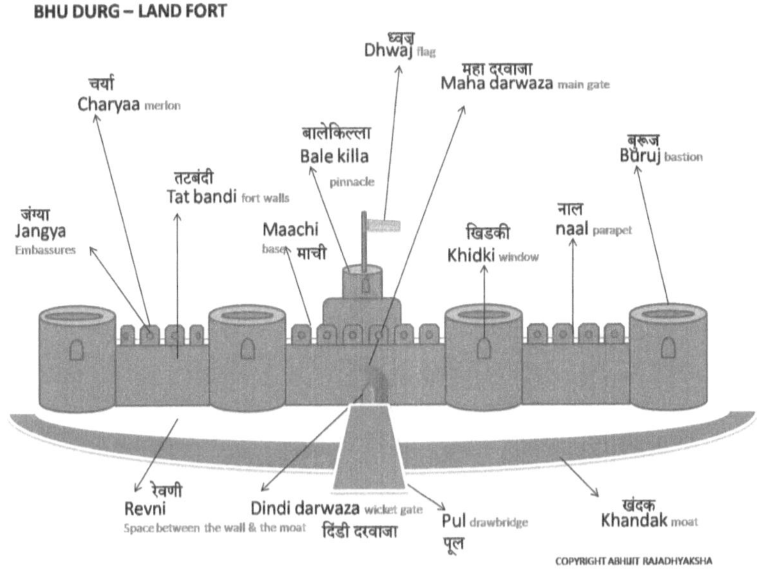

Different parts of Fort (Drawing by Abhijit Rajadhyaksha)

Bastions

Bastions served as watchtowers, with accommodations for guards and storage of cannons. Mounted on wooden carts, cannons could be maneuvered to fire in various directions, offering a wide range of sight and enhanced defense. Circular bastions allowed for effective surveillance and defense in all directions.

Base -Machis

A "Machi" is an essential feature in the construction of forts, especially those with large, flat areas where multiple Machis provide extra security. A Machi is a secure area within the fort surrounded by fortified walls and serves as an outpost for soldiers.

For example, Rajgad Fort has three Machis: Sanjeevani Machi, Padmavati Machi, and Suvela Machi. Pratapgad Fort has Budhla Machi and Zunjar Machi, while the Machi on Korlai Fort is known as "Krusachi Bateri," built by the Portuguese governor in 1551.

Merlon

On the top of the fort walls, solid constructions called Merlon or "Charyas" or "Kangoras" were built. In some forts, these structures, when viewed from a distance, resemble petals of a blooming lotus.

Wallwalk

The protective constructions on top of the fort walls are known as "Fanjis," which include Merlon as well.

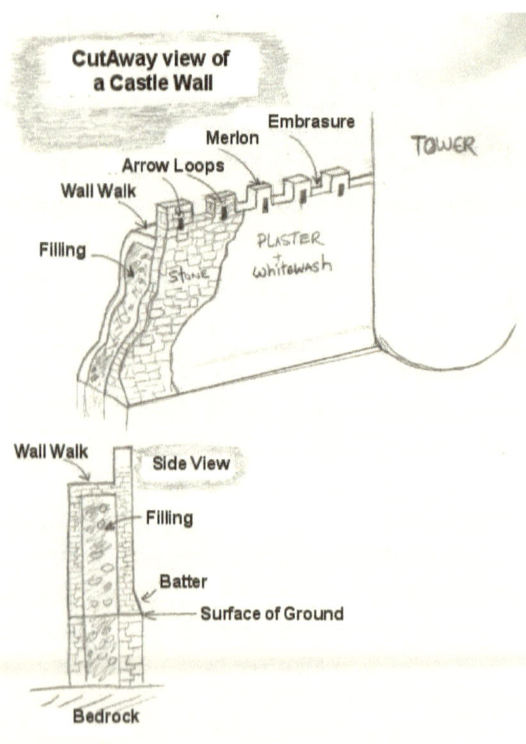

Parts of Fort Wall

Embrasure

The small, square gaps in the fort walls, known as "Jangyas," were designed for shooting gunfire or arrows, keeping watch on enemy movements, and launching attacks from the fort. Jangyas were also present in towers, allowing soldiers to stay protected behind the Fanjis while firing at the enemy through these openings.

Zarokhas or Arrow Loops

Fort walls had loopholes, or "Zarokhas," for gunfire, angled downward. Three nearby loopholes allowed a single person to shoot at three points simultaneously, making it challenging for attackers close to the fort wall. Loopholes are more angled in areas where enemy approach was likely.

Entrance Paths

Forts generally had multiple paths for access, providing alternate routes if one was blocked by enemies. For example, Devgiri Fort had only one entrance route, which forced King Ramdev Rai to surrender when attacked by Alauddin Khilji.

Doors

Forts often had internal doors apart from the main entrance to restrict unauthorized access to various areas. For example, after entering Pratapgad Fort through its Bini Gate, visitors encounter Kothi Gate, Konkan Gate, and Chitta Gate. Shivneri Fort has seven gates, while Mahipatgad has five: Kotwal Gate, Laldeodi Gate, Pusati Gate, Khed Gate, and Shivganga Gate.

Secondary Doors

Aside from the main gate, other doors within the fort are considered secondary gates. On Lohgad Fort, after passing through the last gate, one encounters a winding path with a lower secondary gate and a third gate surrounded by towers, making it difficult for enemies to escape gunfire from Jangyas.

Hidden Doors

Some forts, like Raigad Fort, have secret doors blocked with stones on command. In case the main gate was breached, soldiers could use ropes to escape through these hidden doors. Viratgad and Korlai Fort also have hidden escape paths.

Deceptive Doors

Chakan Fort has a deceptive door. When entering from the east, the path does not lead into the fort but ends at a blank wall, exposing intruders to gunfire from Jangyas.

Wicket Gate

A smaller, lower gate attached to the main gate, known as a "Dindi Gate," required people to bend slightly to pass through.

Tanks and Wells

Forts had numerous tanks, wells, and sometimes a lake for drinking water. These tanks, carved into the rock, were about 5 meters long, 2-4 meters wide, and 8-10 meters deep, filling with rainwater. Sinhagad's "Dev Tank" is famous for its cool, medicinal water, while the tanks on Raigad and Lohgad also have flavorful water. Markinda Fort has three tanks called Kotitirtha (Ramkund), Kamandalu, and Motitank. The Ganga-Jamuna tank is located between the twin forts of Rawlya and Jawlya. Other tanks exist on both forts.

On Purandar Fort, there are two lakes named Rajale and Padmavati, while Mahipatgad has two ponds in the Parashwar Temple complex. Raigad's "Gangasagar" tank, known for never drying, is accompanied by Kushawarta and Hathi lakes, with the Hathi Lake used for elephants.

Citadel

The "Balekilla," or citadel, is the most secure place on the fort, located on the highest point of the peak where the fort is situated. Sometimes, a fort may have two citadels, such as Rajmachi Fort, which has two peaks and thus two citadels with fortified walls in between. Rajgad Fort's citadel is difficult to climb and contains quarters for the fort chief, guards, and occasionally the royal residence.

Sadar (Administration)

The "Sadar" was the administrative area on the fort, where official documentation and tasks were handled. Rajgad Fort has Sadars on all three Machis: Padmavati, Suvela, and Sanjeevani. The fort also had arrangements for horse stables, elephant stables, warehouses for weaponry and grains, making it a self-sufficient village. In case of a siege, these resources were essential for long-term defense.

Ar Killa or Ark Killa

An "Ar Killa" is a small fort found within larger land forts, often mentioned in Persian records as "Kille Ar." Ar Killas are found in place forts (land forts) rather than hill or water forts.

Some distinctive characteristics of medieval forts (Shivaji-era):

Forts such as Pratapgad, Rajgad, Sindhudurg, and Raigad, which were deliberately constructed by Chhatrapati Shivaji Maharaj, and older forts like Sinhagad, Panhala, Janjira, and Devagiri, exhibit a number of contrasting features. Here are some key observations:

1) The primary and external fortifications of hill forts built by Shivaji are typically located around 2/3 of the way up the slope, rather than directly at the hilltop. This placement is significant as the main gate of the fort is also situated at this height. For example, the fortifications surrounding the main gate of Raigad are positioned between Takmak Tok and the Hirakani bastion, approximately 2/3 up the hill. A similar height distinction is seen between the ramparts and the central citadel (Balekilla) at Rajgad, as well as between the Machi (outpost) and Balekilla at Pratapgad.

2) The path approaching the main gate of these hill forts is designed to keep the hill on the right-hand side. During the Shivaji era, fort sieges primarily involved hand-to-hand combat with shields and swords, although firearms, bows, spears, and cannons were also used. However, assaults on the main entrance relied heavily on sword and shield combat. If the path leading to the entrance kept the hill to the right, defenders could exploit this to their advantage. Soldiers stationed on the ramparts could attack with stones, flaming logs, arrows, spears, and bullets, while attackers struggled to use their shields effectively on the left side. This deliberate layout maximizes the defenders' tactical advantage and is a feature unique to forts built by Shivaji, like Raigad and Pratapgad, while absent in older forts such as Sinhagad, Panhala, and Vishalgad.

3) The actual gate of these forts is often concealed and not immediately visible. The exact location of the entrance is difficult to

discern from below.

4) The entrance structure in forts built by Shivaji follows a gomukhi or cow-face design, where the path leading to the main gate is flanked by two bastions, creating a narrow passage. A prime example of this is Raigad's Mahadarwaza (main gate). This design allows defenders to launch attacks on the enemy's rear, while hot oil, water, or stones can be poured on intruders from above. The limited space in front of the gate prevents attackers from retreating far enough to gain momentum for battering rams, limiting their ability to break down the door. The walls are made of carefully laid, seamless stones, making it impossible to wedge anything into gaps. Any cover is minimal, exposing attackers to a constant barrage of bullets, arrows, flaming logs, and spears. This design is an exemplary form of defensive architecture, as reflected in the saying, "It is more likely for Ravana to find a place in Sita's heart than for an enemy soldier to enter through a gomukhi entrance." Raigad has never fallen due to direct assault on the main gate, with power transfers historically occurring only after the garrison's surrender or a treaty.

5) If the main gate is breached, the internal layout continues to impede the enemy's advance with multiple fortifications, checkpoints, and turnarounds that wear down the enemy's morale.

1.4 Summary

Since ancient times, forts have been built across various parts of the world, and their importance grew significantly in the medieval period. In Maharashtra, especially Western Maharashtra with its natural shield of the Sahyadri mountain range, the region became a prime area for fort construction. Maharashtra hosts the highest number of forts in India. Terms like durg (fort) and kila (castle) became commonplace in Marathi, with forts defined by their architectural features and purpose. Numerous treatises, from Kautilya to later writers, outline the importance of forts. Even the city structures of the Harappan civilization bear fort-like designs, indicating the fort's ancient origin. Forts were built with independent, well-equipped layouts, complete with necessities from ramparts to administrative offices, creating a self-sustaining and efficient system.

1.5 Self-Study Questions
Question 1 (Write short answers)
1. Define the various interpretations of forts.
2. List any three parts of a fort.
3. Briefly explain the history of fort construction.
4. What is Citadel?
5. Describe the distinctive features of Shivaji-era forts.
Question 2 (Write notes)
1. Machi
2. Fortifications
3. Revani
1.6 Suggested Reading/Links
1. Forts of Maharashtra
2. Saad Marathwadyatil Killyanchi - Pandurang Patankar
3. Durg Darshan- G. N. Dandekar
4. Durgavidhana - Milind Paradkar
5. Killa-Marathi Vishwakosh
6. http://trekshitiz.com

II

Types and Importance of Forts

Index

2.1 Objectives

2.2 Introduction

2.3 Topic Discussion

1.3.1 Types of Forts

1.3.2 Importance of Forts

2.4 Summary

2.5 Self-Study Questions

2.6 Books for Further Reading

2.1 Objectives

After studying this section, you will:

- Learn the various types of forts.

- Understand the significance of forts in medieval politics.

2.2 Introduction

The construction of forts dates back to ancient times and has varied according to location and purpose, resulting in different types of forts. References to these different types are found across various historical sources, showing changes over time. In the medieval period, only a few types of forts were prominently in use.

Forts were of great importance for the smooth functioning of administration and the protection from enemies. Literature from each era, from Kautilya to Ramachandra Pant Amatya and even the British, highlights the strategic significance of forts. This chapter explores the types and importance of forts.

2.3 Discussion

2.3.1 Types of Forts

The construction of forts has evolved from simple fortifications to strong, defensive structures. Even in the 21st century, for defense against nuclear bombs and other deadly weapons, some protective infrastructures continue to be constructed in the form of forts. Over various eras, based on needs, geographic conditions, and available resources, different types of forts developed. This variety can be seen from the ancient "Pur" of the Vedic period to the modern bunker. Therefore, various historical sources written over time provide descriptions of these distinct types of forts.

In India, fortified cities with citadels were found in the Harappan civilization, dating back to approximately 2300–1750 BCE. However, apart from archaeological remains, no other information is available about the construction of forts or cities from that period. As mentioned in the previous chapter, there is reference to "Pura" from the Rigvedic period, but these were not sturdy constructions. Instead, they were temporary structures with simple enclosures for protection, often made of thorny bushes or rudimentary stone walls. Rigveda describes such settlements as "Pura." The location of the capital was typically naturally protected. If not, artificial fortifications were created around it. The primary goal of all these efforts was to protect wealth and, if necessary, people for a limited time during times of crisis. An invading army could not easily maintain an extended siege due to the difficulty in securing provisions. Even if they tried, the attackers faced the challenge of securing supplies as supply lines were often cut off. Furthermore, invading armies had to retreat by the start of the rainy season due to logistical constraints. Thus, lasting conquests and constant territorial administration were difficult to achieve due to limited manpower and the lack of transport and infrastructure.

By the pre-common era, administrative systems were becoming more advanced in various parts of India, and forts held considerable importance. Some descriptions from the Manusmriti provide insight into the development and uses of forts. Chapter 7 of Manusmriti mentions forts, describing six types of forts as follows: Dhanurdurga, Mahidurga, Abdurga, Radhadurga, Nṛdurga, and Giridurga. These forts had distinct characteristics. For instance, Dhanurdurga referred to a fort with no water within twenty kos (about 75 miles). Mahidurga was a fort with walls at least twelve hands high, along with towers from which soldiers could survey the surroundings. Abdurga, or a water fort, was surrounded by an abundance of water on all sides. Radhadurga was a fort surrounded by thick vegetation like tall trees, thorny bushes, bamboo clusters, and tangled vines. Nṛdurga was a fort guarded by a large infantry equipped with chariots, elephants, and horses, while Giridurga referred to a fort located in the mountains, often surrounded by rivers, springs, and fertile lands for agriculture.

Manusmriti suggests that among these six types, Giridurga (mountain fort) was considered the most secure and advantageous. Each type of fort served a unique purpose, with Dhanurdurga home to deer and similar animals, Mahidurga harboring rodents, Abdurga inhabited by water creatures like fish, crocodiles, and snakes, Radhadurga home to monkeys, Nṛdurga serving as shelter for humans, and Giridurga seen as a dwelling for the divine. Among all these, Giridurga was regarded as superior.

This description reveals that Manusmriti primarily reflects the culture of Aryavarta (the northern region above the Vindhya mountains), where forts in mountainous terrains were prevalent. The architectural styles specific to Maharashtra's Sahyadri and Satpura ranges, especially those made of basalt, were not included in this description. This distinction highlights the regional differences in fort construction and usage.

Compared to the Manusmriti, the Mahabharata provides more detailed information regarding forts and fortifications, particularly in the Shantiparva. According to Bhishma, there is no better stronghold for a king than one resembling a "purusha" (ideal man), and among the six types of forts described in the scriptures, the Nṛdurga (human fort) is considered impregnable. Subsequently, Yudhishthira inquires about the characteristics of a city where a king should reside or how to construct a new one.

In response, Bhishma elaborates, "I will tell you specifically how the forts should be. Listen carefully, and you shall build forts according to this guidance and establish cities under their protection. These forts must be equipped with all kinds of wealth and have adequate space for many people to reside. The types of forts are: Dhanvadurga, Mahidurga, Giridurga, Manushadurga, Mṛdadurga, and Vanadurga. One of these types should serve as a shelter for the royal city. It must always be abundant in grains and weaponry, have strong fortifications, and a robust moat surrounding it. There should be plenty of elephants, horses, and chariots. Skilled artisans should be present, and all kinds of materials must be available. Religious and industrious people should inhabit the area, along with powerful individuals and horses. The city should feature large, beautiful squares and markets, with all transactions conducted openly, ensuring constant peace and the absence of fear. The atmosphere should be vibrant and filled with music."

When it comes to maintaining the fortifications during times of threat from enemies, Bhishma advises: "If you perceive harassment from a king more powerful than yourself, a wise ruler should seek refuge in a fort. The roots of small bushes around the fort should be removed, ensuring that even the leaves of the Ashvattha tree do not fall. It is vital to monitor from the fort's walls where people come from; thus, various watchtowers should be established, guarded by brave individuals. Small holes should be created in the walls for the sentinels to observe outside movements.

In emergencies, these openings should allow for arrow attacks. The moat surrounding the fort should be filled with fish, crocodiles, or have spikes placed strategically within it. To enable citizens to exit in times of crisis, the fort should have secret passages, with sentries stationed at these entrances just like at other gates. Each entrance should be equipped with large gates."

The advancements in architecture are also reflected in Kautilya's Arthashastra. In chapters 24 and 25, titled "Fort Architecture" and "Urban Planning within Forts," considerable details are provided about the architecture of forts and cities. Although this information offers a substantial understanding of the architecture of contemporary forts, it may not be detailed enough for scholars of architecture. Moreover, there are few sources that provide detailed insights into pre-common era architecture. Consequently, the information from Kautilya's Arthashastra becomes quite significant.

Kautilya's guidelines regarding fort architecture state: "Utilize the natural terrain on all sides of your kingdom's borders to construct war-worthy forts. These forts can be surrounded by water, encompassed by a moat, built from stones in hilly regions, or positioned in barren swamps devoid of trees. There are eight types of forts, including those surrounded by water and mountain forts, which protect the country. The barren and forested forts serve as defensive locations or refuges during crises."

For constructing a local (urban) fort for the capital, Kautilya writes: "Establish a city at a confluence of rivers or at the edge of a perennial lake or pond in a spacious area within the central part of the territory. Depending on the location, the layout can be circular, elongated, or rectangular, with water surrounding it on all sides. There should be various marketplaces for different goods, with access routes for both land and water transportation. Surround the city with three moats at a distance of four hands on all sides. The moats should be 14, 12, and 10 dandas wide, respectively, with a depth three-fourths or half of their width. The base should be twice the width of the moat, ensuring it is well-constructed. The sides of the moat should be reinforced with stones or bricks. The moat should contain live water or be filled from an external source. It should have pathways for water drainage and feature lotuses and crocodiles."

A rampart should be constructed from the inner moat to the inner moat, spaced four cubits apart, six cubits high and twelve cubits wide. It should be broad at the bottom and taper at the top, with a bulging middle section. The earth should be filled in and compressed under the weight of elephants and bulls, and thorny trees and poisonous vines should be planted on it. Any holes in the rampart should be filled with fresh earth. Two brick towers should be erected, either twelve cubits or twenty-four cubits tall, at double the height of the rampart. There should be a path for chariots on the rampart, with stones shaped like a talpūl or mṛdunga or resembling the heads of monkeys along its edge. Wood should not be used for this purpose, as it is vulnerable to fire. A platform as high as the rampart should be built every thirty cubits, with a staircase for ascent and descent. Between two platforms on the rampart, a temple should be constructed that is one and a half times the width of the rampart and has two stories with a roof. A window should be protruding enough for three archers to sit between the towers and bastions, with small openings on the window's frame that can be opened or closed as needed.

Secret passages, two cubits wide, should be constructed along the rampart, eight cubits inward from its edge. Inside the rampart, staircases should be built for ascent and descent at intervals of two cubits or four cubits. A retractable bridge should be provided for emergencies to exit the fort, with a secret door near this path.

A concealed path should be created on the outer side of the rampart for exit. This path should be concealed with dangerous items such as barbed stakes, tridents, spikes, serpent bones, palm leaves, sharp weapons, and traps set with wild weapons. Nearby, a stagnant pool of contaminated water should be placed to further conceal the path. There should be arches on both sides of the door, creating a six cubit wide entrance to connect six roads, or the space between the door should range from twenty to thirty cubits, with a height of eight cubits, which is greater than its width by one-sixth or one-eighth. Inside the rampart, there should be a palace, with columns that are between fifteen and eighteen cubits tall. The base of these columns should be one-sixth of their height, and at the tops, one-fourth of their height, with one-third of each column embedded in the ground.

The area of the palace should be divided into five parts. A well should be built in the center, with two long square-shaped platforms on either side of it, and one room at each end of both platforms. Two domed structures should be built outside each platform. A small door should allow access between these structures. The upper section should have two stories, with a height equal to the halfway point of the lower story, and the columns should not be too thick. The area of the third floor should be half or a third of the ground floor area. A spiral staircase should be built in the left corner for ascent to the second and third floors, and other secret staircases should be constructed through the walls. The wooden beam above the main gate should be two cubits thick. The vertical pillars on either side of the door should be three and a fifth cubits thick. Two obstructions should be placed to close the door. The horizontal beam of the door should be five cubits long, with four obstructions to prevent elephants from entering. Near the gatehouse, a mound of earth should be built as wide as the gate's middle and as high as the gate itself. The pathway around the fort should be durable and impassable. Where there is no water around the fort, the path should be on the ground.

The main entrance of the rampart should be decorated with a gate, and in addition to that, a gate resembling a crocodile's mouth should be constructed, one-third the size of the main gate. A stepwell should be built inside the rampart, with an entrance to it provided by a covered passage. A building resembling a kṣatriya should be constructed, twice the area of the gatehouse. Its entrance should be arched and it should not have a roof or pinnacle. Depending on the space and suitability of the weapons and other materials, secret underground storage should be constructed in the fort for weapons, tools, and other equipment. The height should be one-third more than its length and width. The underground storage should contain stone tools, spades, axes, arrows, spearheads, maces, swords, clubs, chakras, and various weapons mentioned earlier that can kill a hundred men in one strike, as well as small arms made by blacksmiths, tridents, spears, curved bamboo sticks resembling a camel's neck, fiery arrows, and numerous other materials mentioned in this context.

Along with the construction of the fort, information regarding the urban planning within this fort, as described by the prevailing architectural practices of the time, is also worth considering. Kautilya states, "The city should be laid out with three roads running east to west and three from north to south, dividing the city into sections. There should be twelve gates to the city, with some accessible from the ground, others via water, and some through underground passages. The common streets of the town should be four cubits wide. The highways, as well as the paths to the market, local areas, districts, military camps, and cemeteries should also be four cubits wide. The path leading to the reservoir and the forest should be four cubits wide. The road to the elephant enclosure should be two cubits wide, while the road for carts should be five cubits wide. The paths for cattle should be four cubits wide and those for sheep, goats, and humans should be two cubits wide.

In the northern part of the city, a strong palace should be built in the newly settled area, where the four castes reside. This should face either north or east. To the northeast of the palace, there should be spaces for the teacher, priest, fire altar, and water storage, as well as residences for ministers. The southeastern part should have a kitchen. On the eastern side, the area should be occupied by merchants of perfumes, flowers, grains, and juices, as well as the residences of skilled artisans and kshatriyas. To the south, there should be a treasury, a jeweler's workshop, and factories.

In the southwestern part, there should be a storage area for wild animals and weapons. To the south of the palace, residences for the mayor, granary manager, trade head, factory head, and military commander should be located, as well as the shops for selling cooked food, fish, and meat, along with spaces for performers and courtesans. In the south of the palace, there should be stables for cows and camels, along with workspace for them. On the western side, artisans should dwell who weave wool and cotton, craft leather, create umbrellas, weapons, and other wares made by shudras. The southwest area should have shops and apothecaries. In the northeastern part, there should be granaries, cow shelters, and horse stables. Beyond that, there should be temples, and the residences of blacksmiths, jewelers, and Brahmins. There should be a space in the center for the local and foreign merchants' association.

In the center of the city, there should be temples dedicated to deities such as Apsavita (Lakshmi), Apratihata (Vishnu), Jayanta (Kartikeya), Vaijayanta (Indra), Shiva, Kubera, Ashwini Kumaras, and Madira (Chamunda). The local deities should be honored and given their rightful place in these temples. Statues of Brahma, Indra, Yama, and Kartikeya should be placed at the gates.

Beyond the trench, at a distance of four hundred hands, there should be sacred tree groves, monasteries, pilgrimage sites, and bridges. Deities associated with the ten directions should be installed according to their respective cardinal points. The cemetery should be located to the north and east of the settlement, with cemeteries designated for higher castes positioned to the south, ensuring they are not encroached upon by others, with fines imposed for violations. Residences for marginalized communities and outcastes should be situated beyond the cemetery. The allocation of land to households should be based on necessity and convenience, with spaces designated for gardens, orchards, and fields as authorized by officials. There should be storage facilities for grain and essential provisions. Wells should be available for every ten households. Items like oil, ghee, salt, grain, medicinal herbs, dried vegetables, parched grains, dried meat, grass, wood, metals, leather, charcoal, bamboo, poisons, horns, reeds, construction timber, assault weapons, and stone projectiles should be stocked in quantities sufficient for several years. As new supplies are obtained, the older stock should be removed.

Officers should be appointed to oversee elephants, horses, chariots, and infantry stationed within the fortress. By assigning multiple officers, each fearing the vigilance of the others, the risk of collusion with enemies is reduced. A similar protocol should be followed for fortresses along border areas. These details provide valuable insight into the social structure of the time, noting the prevalent social hierarchy and caste-based organization.

By Kautilya's era, settlements had become relatively permanent. Although Arthashastra provides a fairly detailed description of fort structures, it focuses on the capital fort alone and omits comprehensive coverage of all fort types, with extensive descriptions confined to administrative setups within the main fort. Kautilya's fort classification expands to include eight distinct types, beyond the earlier six types which had evolved from the original four. Kautilya categorizes these types into four geographic regions: audaka (water fort), parvata (mountain fort), dhanvana (desert fort), and vana (forest fort). Each region contains two subtypes: antadvipa and sthala in audaka; prantara and guha in parvata; nirudakastambha and irana in dhanvana; and davjanodaka and stambhagahana in vana. Given the prevalence of forts on flat lands and the logistical challenges of constructing hill forts in such areas, Kautilya emphasizes nara-durga (man-fortified forts), focusing on fortifications relying on manpower, as the accessible, fertile plains facilitated rapid troop movement and resource mobilization.

The text Abhilashitartha Chintamani suggests that, by the 12th century, fortifications had become essential for a secure and prosperous settlement, with a marked shift towards enduring establishments reflecting societal emphasis on safety and infrastructure. At this time, fort types became categorized based on architectural characteristics and building materials. King Someshvara Deva of Abhilashitartha Chintamani identifies nine fort types:

1. Jaladurg - a water fort naturally surrounded by water.
2. Giridurg - a mountain fort with steep ascents and abundant water sources.

3. Ashmadurg - a stone fort constructed with sturdy rock.

4. Ishtikadurg - a brick and mortar fort surrounded by a trench.

5. Mrittikadurg - a fort made of mud.

6. Vadrhya or Vanadurg - a forest fort shielded by dense, thorny trees like cactus and karvanda.

7. Marudurg - a fort built in an arid, water-scarce region relying on intermittent water sources.

8. Darudurg - a fort with bamboo or timber palisades.

9. Nara-durga - a fort guarded by weaponized soldiers.

Among these, Giridurg and Jaladurg were considered superior, while Darudurg and Nara-durga were deemed inferior, with the remaining types classified as moderate.

Forts constructed on flat terrain are more vulnerable than those in mountainous regions, especially when abundant manpower and natural defenses were not available. In Maharashtra, for instance, the rugged Sahyadri range, with its streams, rivers, and dense forests, inherently provided a defensive barrier against potential invaders, as the monsoon rendered enemy encampments unsustainable. Consequently, forts and deserts within the region were generally safer than the constructed vana or dhanvana forts. Temporary or thorny fencing was used to protect villages from local wildlife and banditry.

In Maharashtra, hill forts (giri-durgas) were particularly abundant, with many adopting features characteristic of forest forts (vana-durgas). The earliest settlers who established hermitages south of the Vindhya Mountains chose secure and water-accessible locations in the mountains, carving out caves, shelters, and rock-cut residences. Later, regional leaders utilized natural mountain fortifications and water sources, ultimately constructing artificial fortifications to enhance these sites' security.

In summary, many forts in Maharashtra were constructed prior to the seventeenth century. Over time, some of these forts fell into disuse or disrepair due to environmental conditions around the mountains. The information in Abhilashitartha Chintamani applies well to Maharashtra, while Varahamihira's Samhita provides insights on water purification suited to southern India. These texts suggest that fortified structures with adequate water resources and robust construction date back as early as the fifth century CE. Forts built under the Bahmani Sultanate and later Muslim rule incorporated local craftsmanship, techniques, and traditional knowledge rather than drawing from exclusively "Islamic" architectural styles. While certain aesthetic preferences of the patrons might reflect Islamic influences, the underlying construction techniques and materials—such as stone masonry—remained rooted in local heritage.

In Shivattvaratnakara, Basavaraja classifies forts into eight types:

1. Mrinmaya (earthen forts),
2. Jalatmika (water forts),
3. Gramakota (village perimeter forts),
4. Guha (cave fortifications),
5. Girikota (hill forts),
6. Bhatwara (citadel or manned fort),
7. Vakra-bhumi (curved or irregular terrain),
8. Vishama (uneven terrain).

In the sixteenth century, another text, Aakashabhairavakalpa, written by a poet associated with the Vijayanagara Empire, describes eight fort types:

1. Giridurg (hill fort),
2. Vanadurg (forest fort),
3. Vaaraksha (fort in dense forest or caves),
4. Jaladurg (water fort),
5. Pankadurg (mud fort),
6. Naabhi (navel-shaped fort in a desert or arid plain),
7. Nara-durg (fort defended by soldiers),
8. Koshthadurg (fort with strong enclosures).

After Shivaji Maharaj's coronation, his minister Raghunathpant Hanamante compiled a lexicon titled Rajyavyavahara Kosha, which includes a dedicated chapter with 26 verses on forest forts, identifying three main types of forts:

1. Giridurg (hill fort),
2. Bhuikot (land fort),
3. Dvipadurg or Janjira (water fort).

Although different texts mention varied classifications, these three types—hill forts, land forts, and water forts—were considered most significant. Medieval sources, especially those focusing on Maharashtra, highlight these three categories, indicating that they were the predominant fort types in the region during this period. Hence, this study will focus on these three fort types in detail.

Giridurg - Hill Fort

According to **Abhilashitartha Chintamani**, a giridurg is a fortress situated on a peak with challenging ascents and ample water sources. **Aakashabhairavakalpa** defines a hill fort as one located on a steep hill with a wide plateau, abundant natural water reservoirs, and multiple layers of protective walls.

Ancient texts like Manusmriti, Shukraniti, and Kautilya's Arthashastra hold hill forts in higher esteem than other fort types. Manusmriti claims, "Among all types of forts, hill forts are the most superior, and thus a king should strive to secure them." The political thinker Shukracharya states, "A single armed man can fight against a hundred warriors within a fortified place, and a hundred soldiers can battle ten thousand men; hence a king should seek refuge in a fort." Kautilya remarks, "Among all types of forts, a water fort is superior to a land fort, but a hill fort is better than a water fort."

During the reign of Shivaji Maharaj, hill forts (giri-durgas) gained significant prominence. The construction, design, and strategic preparation of medieval forts differed from those in ancient times, primarily due to advancements in warfare techniques. Fort protection equated to state protection, necessitating the maintenance of these forts with robust fortifications.

Tikona Fort

New architectural features—such as solid ramparts, bastions capable of absorbing heavy artillery fire, and spaces for cannons and firearms—were incorporated to enhance defensive capabilities. The Sahyadri mountain range, running north to south across Maharashtra, provided ideal high-altitude sites for fortification construction.

Bhuikot - Ground Fort

In **Rajyavyavahara Kosha**, Maharaj refers to a ground fort as *prakar* (encircling wall). **Aakashabhairavakalpa** describes a ground fort as a fortified settlement or town, enclosed by massive walls and protected by surrounding moats. These forts are well-stocked with supplies, such as essential goods, grass, grains, water, and valuables, and are equipped with an array of defensive weaponry, qualifying as a koshta-durga (enclosed fort). In Maharashtra, ground forts are relatively rare but increase in prevalence towards northern regions under Muslim rule.

Ground Fort of Ahemadnagar

Examples of ground forts in Maharashtra, built during the period of Muslim rule, include Paranda, Ahmednagar, Belgaum, Mangalvedha, Miraj, and Solapur.

Jaladurga - Marine Fort

A marine fort, or jaladurga, is constructed on an island within a river or an enduring water body that never dries up. The British, French, Dutch, and Siddis, who were maritime powers, began intervening in Maratha politics, leading to the rise of marine forts along the Konkan coastline. The Murud-Janjira fort, a prominent example, was governed by the Siddis. As the Maratha navy grew, they constructed marine forts on various coastal islets. Maratha-built marine forts include Sindhudurg, Arnala, Vijaydurg, Suvarnadurg, Alibag, Khanderi, Underi, and Padmadurg, while the Siddis constructed the Janjira fort.

Arnala - Sea Fort

In summary, these three primary types of forts—hill forts, ground forts, and marine forts—are found across Maharashtra. However, marine forts are absent in Marathwada, where only hill and ground forts are observed. Additionally, gadhis (small fortifications or minor ground forts) built by regional chieftains are common, functioning as smaller versions of ground forts.

Murud Janjira

2.3.2 Importance of Forts

The construction of forts dates back to ancient times, with the need for fortified structures growing as competition among rulers intensified. As securing territories and protecting trade routes became crucial, the possession of forts translated directly to territorial control. This concept gained prominence during the medieval period when rulers recognized the strategic importance of forts. For instance, the Mughal emperor Akbar constructed forts such as Agra Fort and Fatehpur Sikri with this vision in mind. Similarly, Shivaji Maharaj strategically built and captured numerous forts, underlining the essential role that forts played in state security during the medieval era.

Major Graham, in his report on Kolhapur, aptly identified the role of forts in Maratha politics, stating, "Every fort on the hilltop seems to tell the local people to rely on self-sufficiency rather than depend on their rulers. These forts also instill a spirit of independence in the minds of even minor chieftains, a characteristic unique to the inhabitants of the southern regions of Maharashtra." Likewise, historian Sir Jadunath Sarkar echoed this view in *Shivaji and His Times*, where he wrote, "The Marathas' innate love for independence and seclusion is supported by nature, which has provided them with fortified hills around them. These forts offered immediate refuge and a defensive position from which they could fiercely resist. Unlike the plains of the Ganges, the region could not be easily conquered by a single campaign or prolonged military assault. The residents here were able to engage in prolonged resistance against a superior enemy, often reclaiming their lands once the enemy, exhausted by the conflict, withdrew."

Rajgad

A. Forts as Foundations of the State

During the medieval period, the concept of a state without forts was inconceivable. Thus, the Maratha statesman Ramchandra Bavdekar, in his administrative writings, emphasized the vital role of forts in the establishment of Shivaji Maharaj's Swarajya (self-rule), stating, "Forts are the essence of the entire kingdom. Without forts, the land lies open, vulnerable to enemy invasions, leading to the displacement and distress of the populace. How can a devastated land be considered a kingdom? Historically, every ruler constructed forts to establish a stable territory, using these structures to defend against foreign invasions. Our revered Swami (Shivaji Maharaj) established this holy Swarajya from the forts themselves. In regions lacking self-governance, he strategically built hill forts and marine forts, extending the kingdom unchallenged from the Arikantap to the banks of the Kaveri. Despite the powerful enemy Aurangzeb's advances and attacks on major cities like Bijapur and Golconda, the Marathas withstood these assaults for thirty-two years. While his efforts were relentless, the existence of forts allowed the Marathas to preserve their state, leaving time to consolidate it completely.

For state protection, fort maintenance and reinforcement were paramount. Bavdekar advised establishing new territories by first securing strategically important areas with forts. In regions lacking fortifications, he recommended gradually advancing state boundaries by constructing new forts along the borders, securing them with garrisons, and then extending governance further. Forts provided a foundation for defense, without which prolonged occupation in foreign lands would be unsustainable. In Bavdekar's words, "Forts are the kingdom itself, embodying wealth, military strength, and security." Shivaji Maharaj used these forts to build his state, and it was due to the forts that the Marathas could defend against Mughal invasions. In this sense, Bavdekar's statement, "The essence of the kingdom lies in its forts," succinctly captures the significance of forts.

B. Self-Defense and Military Strategy

Forts were crucial for the defense of the state, as they enabled resistance during enemy invasions. During Shivaji Maharaj's time, these forts held a dual purpose for defense and offensive strategy. Before any campaign, considerations were made about accompanying forces, supplies, and attack routes. In cases of prolonged combat, advancing without first securing enemy-held forts along the path risked compromising supply lines. Thus, such forts would either need to be besieged by Maratha forces or secured to prevent the enemy's soldiers from fleeing. In planning attacks, aspects such as the structure of the troops, routes, and fortifications were essential. Any oversight could result in severe losses. Forts served the primary function of impeding enemy advancements, giving the defenders time to prepare countermeasures. Fortifications were commonly constructed around significant towns to secure valuables and essential resources. These forts also provided refuge for key figures when enemy forces neared.

Certain forts were constructed as tactical bases, allowing nearby forces to provide reinforcements during sieges. In cases where nearby hill forts included areas suitable for mounting cannons, defensive ramparts would be built to prevent the enemy from utilizing them. Some smaller hill forts or gadhis had limited garrisons, yet they could disrupt enemy supply lines. Despite their small size, these forts safeguarded local grain reserves, treasuries, and officials from sudden attacks by local insurgents. During offensive campaigns, forts along the borders provided secure depots for gunpowder and ammunition, as well as fallback positions for retreat if needed.

In the larger forts, the walls typically ranged between 10 to 25 meters in height and 5 to 15 meters in width. These walls were reinforced by constructing both inner and outer walls filled with compressed rubble, topped with mortar to withstand artillery. Parapets with strategically placed openings, known as jangya or bayara, allowed defenders to fire at the enemy while remaining protected.

Shivaji Maharaj utilized the abundant hill forts of Maharashtra to maintain internal order. All forts remained under his direct control, managed by appointed officers who collected state revenue primarily in grain, which was stored in these forts. This grain served as provisions for the army, with payment to soldiers drawn from these resources. The fort officers also managed arms supplies, which were distributed and replenished as needed. This decentralized structure enabled rapid troop mobilization, which exerted pressure on both local rulers and foreign invaders. Ample grain stocks stored securely within forts allowed sustained resistance, ensuring strategic advantage and readiness for multiple years.

Thus, forts not only held strategic military importance but were foundational to the administration and protection of the Maratha state.

The forts played a pivotal role in medieval military, political, and economic frameworks. Each fort secured control over a significant expanse of surrounding territory, effectively placing the area's major trade routes under watch. The presence of stationed troops on these forts allowed for regular patrols along trade routes, ensuring the safe passage of merchants and goods, thus increasing state revenues through trade taxes. Forts such as Shivneri and Salher became instrumental due to their proximity to trade routes, as royal forces could swiftly mobilize to provide security. This security, financed by traders' taxes, further incentivized trade in these regions, enhancing economic prosperity and stability.

Raigad

The state's commitment to trade route protection directly impacted the local populace. Ensuring safe passage on these routes was critical, as theft and ambush were common risks. The existence of forts assured travelers and merchants alike, establishing the fort as a "powerhouse" symbol of stability and control. For instance, Shivaji Maharaj's temporary concession of several forts to the Mughals under the Treaty of Purandar impacted the Marathas' morale, demonstrating how fort control directly correlated with military confidence. Yet, once these forts were reclaimed, the Marathas regained their strategic and psychological advantage.

In addition to safeguarding inland routes, Shivaji Maharaj also prioritized maritime security by fortifying coastal forts, constructing several "sea forts" or "water forts" to protect the burgeoning maritime trade. This strategic foresight countered foreign powers like the Portuguese, French, and British, who used their coastal strongholds to secure maritime dominance. The British, in particular, initially established control over the coastlines by constructing forts, such as Fort St. George in Madras, as early steps to solidify their influence inland. Hence, the fort was not only a military installation but a foundation of the region's economic network, providing local defense and fostering state stability by securing both terrestrial and maritime trade routes.

Fort st. George

In summary, the English, understanding the importance of securing trade routes, traveled thousands of miles to build forts on the western coast of India to protect their trade interests. However, local rulers largely neglected this aspect of trade security. Shivaji

Maharaj recognized this risk and constructed forts like Sindhudurg, but the failure of other rulers to safeguard these routes ultimately led to the loss of both trade and power to the British. This underscores the significance of establishing forts in strategically important locations.

2.4 Summary:

Over time, the types and uses of forts evolved according to the changing needs and circumstances. This adaptation led to variations in fort types in different periods. In ancient times, there were six to nine types of forts, but by the medieval era, only three or four types were commonly used. In Maharashtra, forts from these three categories are predominantly found. The strategic importance of forts also evolved, with their primary purpose in the medieval period being the protection of trade routes, defense of surrounding areas, and safeguarding the kingdom. Ramchandra Pant Amatya, an eminent advisor, aptly emphasized this by stating that "the essence of the state is in its forts."

2.5 Self-study Questions:

Answer the following questions briefly.

1. Explain the types of forts in ancient times.

2. Describe the significance of forts.

3. What are hill forts?

4. What is meant by a "water fort" (Jaldurg)?

5. Define "land fort" (Bhuikot).

2.6 Suggested Reading/Links

1. Forts of Maharashtra

2. Saad Marathwadyatil Killyanchi - Pandurang Patankar

3. Durg Darshan- G. N. Dandekar

4. Durgavidhana - Milind Paradkar

5. Killa-Marathi Vishwakosh

6. http://trekshitiz.com

III

Forts of Marathwada: Hill Forts

Index

3.1 Objectives

3.2 Introduction

3.3 Topic Discussion

3.3.1 Hill forts of Marathwada

3.3.2 Hill forts in Chh. Sambhajinagar (Aurangabad) District A. Vetalwadi B. Vaishagad C. Antur D. Pedka E. Sutonda F. Lahugad G. Devgiri H. Bhangshi

3.3.3 Hill forts in Jalna District - A. Rohilgad

3.3.4 Hill forts in Parbhani District - A. Nemgiri 3.3.5 Hill forts in Nanded District - A. Mahur

3.4 Summary

3.5 Self-Study Questions

3.6 Books for Further Reading

3.1 Objectives

After studying this unit, you will:

- Gain insight into the hill forts of Marathwada

- Acquire district-wise information on the forts of Marathwada

3.2 Introduction

The region of Marathwada is primarily known for its hill forts and land forts (Bhuikot). During the medieval period, the Yadavas controlled Marathwada until it later came under the authority of the Delhi Sultanate. When the Sultanate weakened, its governance was overtaken by the Bahmani Sultanate. Following its division, five states emerged, including parts of Nizamshahi and Qutbshahi in Marathwada. Eventually, this region fell under the Mughal empire after the decline of Nizamshahi. While the Marathas prioritized hill forts, other ruling powers did not emphasize them to the same extent. The geographical landscape of Marathwada is not highly favorable for hill forts, with no continuous mountain ranges like the Sahyadri, aside from the Ajanta mountain range in Chhatrapati Sambhajinagar District and the Balaghat range in Beed District. Despite this, hill and land forts are found in significant numbers.

3.3 Discussion of the Topic

3.3.1 Hill Forts of Marathwada

The geographical backdrop of Marathwada, including the Satmala-Ajanta mountain range extending from west to east in the northern region, is a distinctive feature. Consequently, most hill forts in Marathwada are located along this range, especially in Chhatrapati Sambhajinagar District, which contains 8 of Marathwada's 11 major hill forts. The remaining three hill forts are scattered across the other seven districts, with Beed, Dharashiv (Osmanabad), Latur, and Nanded districts lacking any hill forts.

The prominent hill forts in Marathwada are as follows:

1. Vetalwadi
2. Vaishagad
3. Antur
4. Pedka
5. Sutonda
6. Lahugad
7. Devgiri (Daulatabad)
8. Bhangshi [all located in Chhatrapati Sambhajinagar District]
9. Rohilgad (in Jalna District)
10. Jintur (in Parbhani District)

11. Mahur (in Nanded District)

The average elevation of the mountain ranges in Marathwada is lower than that of the Sahyadri, and the region receives less rainfall than Western Maharashtra, Konkan, and Vidarbha. Consequently, the forts here are less inaccessible than those in the Sahyadri. Additionally, due to lower rainfall, it was feasible to inhabit these forts even during the monsoon season.

3.3.2 Hill Forts of Chhatrapati Sambhajinagar (Aurangabad) District

The particular geographic structure of Marathwada, including the west-east extension of the Satmala-Ajanta range, which lies to the north of Marathwada and Chhatrapati Sambhajinagar District, influences the distribution of forts. The discontinuous nature of this range results in the isolation of forts in this district. However, this range contributes to the high concentration of hill forts, with eight of Marathwada's total eleven hill forts located in Chhatrapati Sambhajinagar District. Information on these forts is provided below:

A. Vetalwadi Fort

Located only 3 kilometers from Halda village in Soygaon Taluka, Vetalwadi Fort is locally referred to as Vasai Fort or Wadi Fort. According to some historians, this fort was constructed by the Gupta dynasty's King Vikramaditya in the 6th century. However, the Archaeological Department notes that it was built in the 12th century, with some scholars attributing it to the Chalukya or Yadava periods. Lacking evidence such as inscriptions or coins, there is still uncertainty regarding the fort's origins. It is speculated that after the 15th century, the fort was controlled by the rulers of Ahmednagar, then by the Mughals, and later by the Nizam of Hyderabad, although the precise creator and time of construction remain unknown due to insufficient evidence.

Vetalwadi Fort

Located on the boundary between Soygaon and Sillod Talukas, Vetalwadi Fort can be found on the left when heading from Vetalwadi towards Halda Village via the mountain pass road. From the mountain pass, a path leads up to the fort. This fort, situated on the highest point of the Ajanta mountain range, has its main northern-facing gate called the "Janjala Gate," oriented towards Janjala Fort. There is also a second gate, known as the "Wadi Gate," which faces the base village of Vetalwadi. Both gates are approximately 20 feet high and display intricate carvings on their pillars. Inside the main gate, there are shelters for guards. Upon entry, a domed structure is visible within the fort, along with the remnants of a grand bastion, turrets, rooms for grain storage, stables, oil and ghee reservoirs, the Namjagir Mosque, a dilapidated palace, and a cannon that measures 6 feet 10 inches in length, all of which remain well-preserved.

Arches of Vetalwadi fort

B. Vaishagad / Janjala / Taltam Fort

Vaishagad, a fort of considerable size, is constructed atop a mountain in the Satmala-Ajanta mountain range. Also known as Taltam Fort, this fort is called "Sonkilla" or "Lalkilla" by locals. Historians disagree on its exact origin, though it is believed to date back to the Vakataka period in the 5th century CE. The ancient name of Janjala village was Jinjala, as mentioned in inscriptions found in the Ghatotkach caves, which reference a princess from the Ashmaka kingdom. The minister Varahadeva, of the Vakataka king, is credited with excavating these caves in the 5th century CE. In 1553 CE, Burhan Nizam Shah of Ahmednagar conquered the fort, and it later fell to Shah Jahan in 1631. Despite limited historical records, the fort contains numerous architectural remains. There is a tomb for the saint Syed Al Kabir Qadri, and inscriptions in Persian adorn the entrance.

Vaishagad

C. Antur Fort

Strategically situated on the east-west extension of the Sahyadri mountains within the Ajanta-Satmala range, Antur Fort lies in Kannad Taluka of Chhatrapati Sambhajinagar District. Designated as a protected monument by the Maharashtra Department of Archaeology, this solid and robust fort was initially built by a Maratha chieftain. Later, it fell under the rule of Ahmednagar's Nizam Shahi dynasty, during which some construction was undertaken under Malik Ambar's guidance. The fort was subsequently overtaken by the Mughals and later claimed by the British, along with other forts in the region.

On the eastern side of Antur, a cliff faces south, where a visually striking gate is nestled. Its narrow placement makes it difficult to notice until approached directly. There are guard posts situated outside this gate, and until recently (up to 1990), this gate featured wooden doors, which have since disappeared. Beyond this entryway, an interior passage is enclosed by fortified walls and remains narrow, with many fallen stones along its length. Another, larger gate faces east; crossing this gate leads to a third entryway, whose interior archways feature intricate carvings. These carvings, along with ornamental cannonballs used for decoration, are unique in Maharashtra and rare beyond its borders. The third gate bears a grand inscription in Persian, situated near the central area of the fort.

Antur Fort

The fort spans a north-south axis, enclosed by fortified walls. As one moves toward the northern end along the perimeter, turrets are visible within the fortifications. To the left lies a hill with a large reservoir on its southern slope, and a grand building on the hillside, accessible via stairs. Atop the hill, a substantial watchtower with northern-facing steps offers a strategic vantage point for monitoring the entire fort and viewing the Ajanta-Satmala range, as well as Khandesh to the north. The southern part of the fort is enclosed by a separate wall with three gates, the largest of which is flanked by two turrets to the south. On the western slope of the central hill, near the fortifications, a water tank is carved. The northern part of the fort resembles a citadel and has been reinforced. The fort connects to the mountain range on its northern side, where a deep moat is carved out, its upper edge fortified by a robust wall featuring a defensive structure.

D. Pedka Fort

Another fort in the Satmala-Ajanta mountain range, Pedka Fort, has largely fallen into obscurity. Very little information is available regarding this fort, which is believed to have been built before the Yadava dynasty. Devgiri, located in Chhatrapati Sambhajinagar District, was the capital of the Yadavas, and during their rule, a network of forts was established for surveillance on routes leading to the capital. Following the defeat of the Yadavas, the strategic importance of Devgiri diminished, along with that of its surveillance forts. Consequently, some forts, particularly those in remote locations, faded into oblivion. Pedka Fort, located in Kannad Taluka of Chhatrapati Sambhajinagar District, is one such example.

E. Sutonda Fort

Located on an isolated hill within the Ajanta-Satmala range in Soygaon Taluka of Chhatrapati Sambhajinagar District, Sutonda Fort is notable for its extensive caves and unfinished water tanks. The architectural features suggest it dates back to antiquity, likely the 4th or 5th century CE. Among the caves, an image of Lord Mahavira and statues of Yaksha and Yakshini are visible, suggesting that the fort may have been used for reconnaissance or as a decoy structure to mislead enemies, rather than for permanent habitation. The abundance of water tanks also raises questions about the purpose of such extensive provisions. Based on the fortified structure above the subterranean gate, the fortifications likely date back to the Bahmani period, and following the division of the Bahmani Sultanate in the 16th century, the fort came under Nizam Shahi control. The Badshahnama, a Mughal chronicle, records that in 1630-31 CE, the Mughal commander Sipahandar Khan attacked Sutonda Fort on the orders of Emperor Shah Jahan, compelling the fort's commander, Siddi Jamal, to surrender. The British Gazette of Aurangabad references this fort as "Saitenda," noting its location 26 miles northeast of Kannad. It also mentions that Emperor Aurangzeb granted sanads (land grants) to certain Deshmukhs for the fort.

Sutonda

F. Lahugad Fort

Lahugad Fort, located in Phulambri Taluka of Chhatrapati Sambhajinagar District, has an unknown history. Its proximity to Devgiri and the presence of rock-cut tanks and caves suggest a construction date in the 7th or 8th century CE. Chhatrapati Sambhajinagar District is home to remarkable rock-cut structures such as the Ajanta and Verul caves, as well as the Devgiri Fort, renowned for its intricate rock architecture. Lahugad aligns with these structures as a small but unique rock-cut fort approximately 40 kilometers from Chhatrapati Sambhajinagar city. The fort features a rock-carved temple, 18 water tanks of various types, rock-cut gates, staircases, and caves, showcasing diverse sculptural forms. Situated along the ancient routes from Aurangabad to Ajanta and from Aurangabad to Jalna, this fort appears to have been established to monitor the pass connecting these two routes, which runs parallel to the Ajanta mountain range.

Lahugad

G. Daulatabad Fort (Devagiri)

This is a well-known hill fort located in the Sambhajinagar taluka. The fort hill rises to a height of 600 feet and is surrounded by a 50-foot wide moat filled with water. The cliff from the base of the moat to about 150 to 200 feet high has been so precisely carved that even a snake would find it impossible to climb up.

Upon entering through the main gate, on the right side stands a tower called "Chand Minar." This minaret was built in the 15th century, around 1435 AD, by Alauddin Bahmani after he captured the fort. The tower is 210 feet tall with a base circumference of 70 feet and consists of four floors. In the same area, there is a cannon known as "Kille Shikan" (Fort Breaker), also called "Mendha Cannon." It is made of a five-metal alloy. Nearby, there is a Hemadpanti temple with 180 columns, where a statue of Bharat Mata (Mother India) was installed by the local people in 1950. In front of this temple is an extensive water reservoir named Hathi Hauz, measuring 150 feet in length, 100 feet in width, and 23 feet in depth.

Devgiri/ Daulatabad

Before the establishment of the current fort, Daulatabad (Devagiri) emerged as a significant religious and trading center. Positioned on an ancient trade route, this site was home to early caves and rock-cut dwellings, predominantly Jain and Shaiva. Recognizing its strategic importance, a fort was constructed here, likely during the Rashtrakuta era in the 8th century. However, the fort we see today reflects subsequent modifications. Between 1150 and 1300, the Yadava rulers made this their capital, constructing the great fortification wall (Mahakot) and building Hindu temples.

Later, the Delhi Sultanate captured the site, marking the end of Yadava rule and the beginning of Khalji-Tughlaq dominance. Malik Kafur, a general under Alauddin Khalji, invaded in 1308-1313, significantly altering the fort's history. Using columns from destroyed temples, Qutb-ud-din Mubarak Khalji constructed the Jama Masjid. Sultan Muhammad bin Tughlaq, after declaring

Daulatabad his capital, ordered the relocation of people from Delhi and initiated the construction of a new stone wall with round bastions. For the newly settled Delhi population, a fortified settlement was established in the Amarkot area, and water channels around the hill were utilized for defensive moats.

Chand Minar at Daulatabad Fort

During the Bahmani period (1350–1450), Daulatabad was transformed into a crucial military base. The inner citadel was reinforced, and a moat (10 meters wide and 16 meters deep) was carved around the rock at its base. Ahmad Shah Bahmani erected the Chand Minar in 1435, and the Rang Mahal was also built in this era. From 1450 to 1650, during the Nizam Shahi period, additional palatial structures were built, including fortifications in the Mahakot wall and improved water management systems. Remnants from the Mughal period (1650–1750) include the well-preserved Baradari and ruins of a palace within Mahakot. The Marathas took control from 1750 to 1800, leaving behind a partially intact Shiva temple within Mahakot.

H. Bhangshi Fort

Located approximately 14-15 kilometers from Sambhajinagar city, this fort sits on a secluded hill, part of the Ajanta range, with a temple dedicated to Bhansai Mata, giving the fort its name, Bhanshi Fort. Although historical records are sparse, ancient caves here suggest that the hill was used for religious purposes long before the fort was constructed. Given its proximity to Devagiri, Bhanshi Fort likely served a strategic role for defense or reconnaissance. Today, remnants of the fort's walls and structures can still be seen.

Bhangsi Gad

3.3.3 Hill Forts of Jalna District
Rohilgad Fort

Located near Rohilagad village in Ambad Taluka of Jalna district, this is the sole hill fort in the area. Although limited historical information is available, evidence of ancient rock-cut caves suggests its early utilization. Its strategic location along an old trade route likely provided protection to nearby market towns like Ambad and

Jalna. The fort's name is believed to derive from the "Rohila" people (from Rajasthan or Afghanistan) who once inhabited the region.

3.3.4 Hill Forts of Parbhani District

Jintur/Nemgiri Fort

This lone hill fort, located near Jintur village, is also known as Nemgiri Fort and holds significance as a Jain pilgrimage site. Now largely in ruins, only fragments of the fort's walls and bastions remain. The hill features seven interconnected Jain caves containing idols of Jain Tirthankaras, with the notable "Antariksha Parshvanatha" statue in the fifth cave—a 6-foot statue, weighing around 9-10 tons, reputedly suspended in mid-air in earlier times. These caves likely date back to the Rashtrakuta period. Local lore suggests that Jintur was previously named Jainpur, later evolving into its present name.

Nemgiri Fort

3.3.5 Hill Forts of Nanded District

Mahur Fort

Situated in the Mahur taluka of Nanded district, Mahur Fort, previously known as Ramgad Fort, is the sole hill fort in the district. The area around Mahur village hosts Hindu caves dating back to the 8th-9th centuries, often referred to as "Pandava Caves." During the Rashtrakuta period, this village was known as "Mahapur," which later evolved into "Mahur." Near Mahapur village, the hill containing Ramgad Fort eventually became known as "Mahur Fort." In the Yadava period, this fort served as an administrative center, though it passed into the hands of the Gond kings in the 14th century.

Mahur Fort

In 1350, Sultan Hasan Shah launched an attack on the fort, which was preserved through a ransom payment. In 1412, the Bahmani Sultanate attempted another siege, yet failed to capture it. However, in 1422, Sultan Ahmed Shah Wali of the Bahmani Sultanate successfully took the fort by launching a surprise attack, executing Gond King Jayasingh and his army. Renaming the fort "Ahmedabad," he established it as the primary military station for southern Vidarbha, appointing Khudawand Khan as its governor. However, Khudawand Khan rebelled against Bahmani rule, leading to his eventual defeat and death at the hands of Bahmani subedar Amir Barid. Subsequently, Imad Shah included the fort in his kingdom, until it was later captured by the Nizam. In 1529, Mughal Emperor Akbar seized the fort from the Nizam, entrusting its maintenance to Udajiram, whose descendants remained chiefs of the fort for several generations. In 1658, Jagjivanram was the fort keeper, followed by his son Baburao, under the regency of his mother, Savitribai. When the fort faced an attack by Harchanda Rajput, Savitribai heroically defended it, for which Aurangzeb honored her with the title "Pandita Raybaghan."

During the 18th century, the Nagpur Bhosales seized the fort from the Mughals, only for it to be later reclaimed by the Nizam. The fort remained under Nizam control until India's independence.

In Marathwada's eight districts, only Sambhajinagar, Jalna, Parbhani, and Nanded possess hill forts; the remaining four districts—Beed, Hingoli, Dharashiv, and Latur—lack such fortifications. This chapter provides detailed accounts of 11 out of 23 known hill forts in Marathwada.

3.4 Summary

Marathwada's hill forts, found primarily along the Satmala-Ajanta ranges and determined by district-specific geography, offer a rich historical perspective. Sambhajinagar district, with its west-to-east stretching mountain range, naturally holds the highest number of hill forts, totaling eight, although not all are widely recognized. Jalna, Parbhani, and Nanded each have one hill fort, underscoring Marathwada's historical and strategic development. This information contributes to a deeper understanding of the region's historical and cultural heritage.

3.5 Self-study Questions

Question 1 Answer the following questions:

A. Name any five hill forts in Marathwada.

B. Which district in Marathwada has the highest number of hill forts, and why?

Question 2: Write brief notes on:

a) Devgiri

b) Mahur

c) Nemgiri

3.6 Suggested Reading/Links

1. Forts of Maharashtra
2. Saad Marathwadyatil Killyanchi - Pandurang Patankar
3. Durg Darshan- G. N. Dandekar
4. Durgavidhana - Milind Paradkar
5. Killa-Marathi Vishwakosh
6. http://trekshitiz.com

IV
Forts of Marathwada: Ground Forts

Index

4.1 Objectives

4.2 Introduction

4.3 Topic Discussion

4.3.1 Ground Forts of Marathwada

4.3.2 Ground Forts in Chh. Sambhajinagar (Aurangabad) District

A. Fardapur Sarai B. Ajintha C. Ajintha Sarai D. Kile Ark

4.3.3 Ground Forts in Beed District A. Dharur B. Dharmapuri

4.3.4 Ground Forts in Parbhani & Hingoli District A. Pathri (Parbhani) B. Pethwadgao (Hingoli)

4.3.5 Ground Forts in Nanded & Latur District A. Nanded B. Kandhar (Nanded) C. Ausa D. Udgir (Latur) 4.3.5 Ground Forts in Dharashiv District A. Paranda B. Naldurg

4.4 Summary

4.5 Self-Study Questions

4.6 Books for Further Reading

4.1 Objectives

After studying this unit, you will:

• Gain knowledge about Marathwada's land forts.

• Access district-wise information about the land forts in Marathwada.

• Understand Marathwada's historical trajectory.

4.2 Introduction

Marathwada holds a vast historical and cultural legacy. Just as the forts of Maharashtra reflect the state's historical development, so too do the forts of Marathwada. This region's historical importance is recorded as far back as the Maurya period and the Mahajanapada era, establishing Marathwada as a land of rich historical significance. The region's land forts, in particular, represent this legacy. In this section, we will examine the land forts of Marathwada in detail.

4.3 Topic Discussion

4.3.1 Land Forts of Marathwada

Though Marathwada has fewer forts compared to the Sahyadri Mountains of western Maharashtra, and they may lack the same ruggedness, the variety and grandeur of Marathwada's forts still stand out, particularly the land forts. In fact, Marathwada has almost as many land forts as hill forts, if not more. Excluding the Devgiri Fort, most hill forts in Marathwada are smaller and less challenging. However, the land forts are especially notable for their size and impressive structure, and Marathwada could be regarded as famous for its land forts just as western Maharashtra is for its hill forts.

Marathwada hosts a total of 25 forts, 11 of which are hill forts, and the remaining 14 are land forts. Every district in Marathwada has land forts, with the exception of Jalna. In the following sections, we will provide district-wise information on each of these land forts.

4.3.2 Land Forts in Sambhajinagar (Aurangabad) District

A. Fardapur Sarai

Located near the Ajanta caves, the village of Fardapur lies along the Ajanta mountain pass. A strategic arrangement was made with Ajanta Sarai at the top of the pass and Fardapur Sarai at the bottom, situated on the main road toward Aurangabad. These serais (Persian for "palace" or "inn") served as rest stops for the military or high-ranking officials such as subedars (often royal princes) or prominent noblemen traveling with the army, as well as for defense and security checkpoints. The construction of this sarai is likely from Aurangzeb's era, although there are no definitive records. This grand, fortified land fort retains well-preserved bastions, ramparts, and a main gate with wooden doors still intact.

Entrance gate of Fardapur Sarai

B. Ajanta Fort

Close to the famed Ajanta caves in Sambhajinagar district is the village of Ajanta. This village, on the banks of the Waghur River, was once enclosed within the walls of a land fort. The fort's ramparts can be seen along the river's edge, though they are now fragmented due to village expansion. Likely built during the Mughal period, this expansive land fort includes multiple gates and more than 30 bastions, which protected a market within. With impressive Mughal architecture, Ajanta Fort is a complete land fort and a fine example of medieval military architecture.

Ajanta Fort

C. Ajanta Sarai

This sarai, along with Fardapur Sarai, lies along a pass road that provided security and temporary accommodations for travelers. The Ajanta land fort and both serais were likely constructed in the Mughal era.

Ajanta Sarai

D. Qil'a Ark

Qil'a Ark, located in the heart of Chhatrapati Sambhajinagar city, is an earthen fortification and a notable example of Mughal architecture. The city of Khadki was originally established by Malik Ambar, who constructed structures like the Naukhanda Palace and the Bhadrakali Gate. However, during the two stages of Mughal Emperor Aurangzeb's tenure in the Deccan region, major architectural landmarks such as the Qil'a Ark and the renowned Bibi ka Maqbara were developed. While the Bibi ka Maqbara is well-known, the Qil'a Ark served as a residential fortification built by the Mughal Emperor himself. The word "Ark" is derived from the Turkish language, meaning "residence," suggesting that Qil'a Ark was a "fortified residence," as interpreted by Dr. Dulari Qureshi.

Naubat Darwaja

Emperor Aurangzeb began construction on this fort in 1653 when he was the Governor of the Deccan. The construction completed between 1656 and 1659, but Aurangzeb didn't reside there until his return to the Deccan in 1681 after securing the Mughal throne. During his stay, the administration of India was managed from this fort. At that time, Aurangabad (now Chhatrapati Sambhajinagar) was a walled city, remnants of which can still be seen near the Kham River. The city's gateways, such as the historical ones still present, connected these fortifications, indicating that the entire city was once confined within these walls, although it later expanded beyond them.

Aurangzeb, along with his family, resided in this fort for many years. A mosque, the Shahi Masjid, was built within the fort for the royal family, where Aurangzeb, despite being the ruler of India, would engage in the humble act of cap-weaving. Aurangzeb's son's wedding was also held within the fort. The fort housed separate residential areas, with the Zenana Mahal for royal women, the Mardana Mahal for men, and an exclusive mosque for the royal women to offer prayers. The fort's walls, extending from the Delhi Gate to the Amkhas Maidan, were equipped with numerous towers, and several gates such as Kala Darwaza, Rangi Darwaza, and Adil Darwaza, which are still visible today. The Zenana Mahal is a rare architectural marvel in Maharashtra, with only a few similar structures.

Kile Ark - Janana Mahal (late 19th century photograph)

In the Nizam's era, the fort came under the Nizam's rule, and various offices began operating within it. Marathwada's first college, founded by the Nizam in 1923, known today as the Government College of Arts and Sciences, also resides within this fort complex.

4.3.3 Ground Forts in Beed District

A. Dharur Fort

The ancient city of Pratishthan (Paithan), once the capital of the Satavahana dynasty, was well-connected, with trade routes passing through places like Dharur, which developed as a commercial hub. During the Rashtrakuta dynasty, a fort was built here. Initially known as "Mahadurga" after the deity Dhareswar, this fort was built using ordinary stones. The Rashtrakuta king Govind III (793–814 CE) mentions Dharur in one of his donation records. Over time, the region came under the rule of the Kalyani Chalukyas and then the Yadavas of Devagiri.

After the Yadava Empire fell, Dharur flourished as a trade center under the Bahmani Sultanate, which moved its capital to Bidar in 1422. This move increased Bidar and nearby Udgir's significance. The Bahmani kingdom eventually split into five independent sultanates, including the Barid Shahi Sultanate, with its capital at Bidar. Dharur, Udgir, Ausa, and Kandhar were the major forts in the Barid Shahi territory, which often clashed with the Adil Shahi, Nizam Shahi, and Qutb Shahi dynasties due to territorial disputes.

Following the decline of the Barid Shahi dynasty, intense conflict over Dharur Fort occurred between the Adil Shahi and Nizam Shahi dynasties. Recognizing its strategic importance, Adil Shahi architect Kishwar Khan Lari renovated the fort in 1567 using stones from Mahadurga. However, this project escalated tension with the Nizam Shah, who attacked the fort in 1569, seizing it and renaming it Fatehabad.

In 1601, the Mughals captured Ahmednagar, leading to the collapse of the Nizam Shahi dynasty. Subsequently, the Mughal general Azam Khan took control of Dharur Fort in 1630–31, commemorating the victory with a specially minted coin. Dharur's coin mint operated for nearly a century afterward.

During the Battle of Panhala, differences arose between Shivaji Maharaj and his general Netaji Palkar, who later joined the Mughals and resided in Dharur Fort. After Shivaji's escape from Agra, Palkar was held in Dharur Fort on Emperor Aurangzeb's orders.

Fort of Dharur

In 1760, at the Battle of Udgir, Maratha leader Sadashivrao Bhau decisively defeated the Nizam's forces. However, the Nizam's reinforcements sought refuge in Dharur Fort. After the battle of Kharda, the Marathas briefly controlled Dharur Fort before it returned to the Nizam's possession. It remained under Nizam rule until India's independence.

B. Dharmapuri

Ambajogai, an ancient village in Beed district, is renowned for its Brahmani (Hindu) caves and the Yogeshwari Temple. Approximately 27 km from Ambajogai lies Dharmapuri, a significant historical religious site. This village hosts the ancient Kedareswar Temple, which dates back to the Chalukya era. During the Bahmani or Mughal period, a fort was constructed here, now known as the Dharmapuri Fort. The stones used in its construction contain remnants of sculptural carvings, suggesting that several temples once existed in the area, and stones from these temples were likely repurposed in building the fort. Both the Dharmapuri Fort and the intricately carved Kedareswar Temple are notable sites worth visiting.

Fort of Dharmapuri

4.3.4 Forts in Parbhani and Hingoli Districts
A. Pathri (Parbhani)

Pathri, originally named Parthpur, is an ancient site. The Pathri Fort, though mostly in ruins, has two wells and remnants of two gates. Records in the Maharashtra state archives mention that around six centuries ago, a structure on the fort premises was converted into the Shah Hamid Uddin Dargah. This dargah (shrine) is octagonal in shape, featuring twelve pillars and a dome of approximately 9.5 meters in height. Each corner has large pillars, with the structure's interior adorned with intricate carvings displaying Hindu artistic influences. The dargah has four entrances, three of which are now closed off, and the surrounding walls are punctuated with arrow slits.

Pathri's name evolved from Parthpur, and references indicate that a temple dedicated to Arjuna (Parth Temple) was once here. The well-known writer Sant Shridhar authored the "Gemini

Ashwamedha" text in this village.

This fort, though in ruins, retains parts of its original structure. The dargah within, known as Shah Hamid Umid Dargah, is believed to have been constructed on a structure dating back about 600 years. The dargah features twelve pillars supporting a dome, with intricate carvings inside reflecting Hindu artistic motifs. It has four entrances, of which three are closed.

Dargah of Syed Shah Ismail Sahib Qadi Built around 200 years ago, this dargah becomes a focal point during the Ramadan month for the annual fair (Urs).

Dargah of Syed Sadar, also known as Aminoddin Shah Rafi Dargah (the Great Dargah), This dargah, around 725 years old, is connected to a mosque and has four entry points, with the main door being the largest. The structure is stone-built, with the upper portion made of bricks. There is a well to the left of the mosque, built in 1334 Hijri (Islamic calendar). The main gateway has an upper floor with four minarets.

B. Pethwadgaon (Hingoli)

The Shiv-era Pethwadgaon Fort in Hingoli district (Kalmanuri taluka) attracts school students due to its historical legacy. Nava Saji Naik, who challenged both the Nizam and the British, also stayed here for a while. Formerly, Fort Wadgaon and Pethwadgaon were parts of a single territory known as Kille Wadgaon, which later divided, placing the fort under Pethwadgaon's jurisdiction. The fort is surrounded by four bastions and contains various underground passages. An inscription in medieval script can also be found on one of the fort's stones.

Numerous historical events are associated with the fort. Previously, a woman named Raybagan managed the fort's administration. During the 1857 revolt, Nava Saji Naik, a prominent leader who led an uprising against the British for over twenty years, briefly stayed here. Local villagers recount that after being cornered by British forces at Navha village, Naik escaped through an underground passage and sought refuge in this fort.

Pethwadgaon Fort

4.3.5 Forts in Nanded and Latur Districts
A. Nanded

References to Nanded can be found as far back as the Maurya Empire, around the 6th century BCE. Historically known by names like Nanditatt, Nandinagar, and Nandigram, this city was established by a king from the Nanda dynasty. Paithan served as the capital of the Nanda dynasty in southern India, with Nandahaar and Navnanddera as subsidiary capitals. The name "Nanded" is derived from the transformation of Navnanddera. Being a subsidiary capital and trade center, it was natural for Nanded to have fortifications for its protection. Nanded was a fortified town.

During the Satavahana period, Nanded became an important Buddhist learning center, and references to it are found in the donation inscriptions at the Sanchi Stupa. Later, during the reigns of the Vakatakas, Chalukyas, Rashtrakutas, and Ganga rulers, Nanded flourished as a prominent educational hub and a wealthy city. Subsequently, under the Bahmani, Mughal, and finally Nizam rule, the fort remained under their control, preserving the significance of Nanded.

B. Kandhar (Nanded)

This fort in Nanded district is relatively well-preserved. In the 7th century CE, King Krishna I of the Rashtrakuta dynasty made Kandhar the capital. Around that time, a lake named Jagattunga Samudra was constructed for Kandhar's water supply, and the fort was built. In the 9th century, Chalukya King Gunaga Vijayaditya III set Kandhar on fire, but Rashtrakuta King Krishna III restored it and strengthened the fort. King Krishna III constructed the fort along the banks of the Manyad River in the 10th century CE. Subsequent dynasties added to the fort's architecture, with modifications and expansions continuing up to 1840. The oldest enduring structure within the fort is a stepwell from the Yadava period. At the main gate, Persian carvings from the time of Muhammad Tughlaq (1325-1351) are visible. After the 13th century, the Bahmani Sultanate made significant additions to the fort, which had a unique multi-layered defense system that kept it secure for centuries.

Ground Fort of Kandhar

In 1347, Muhammad Tughlaq captured the fort and appointed Nasrat Sultan as the fort's keeper. After the formation of the Bahmani Sultanate, the fort came under their rule. In 1565, the Ahmadnagar Nizamshahi took control of the fort, but Chand Bibi later handed it over to the Mughals. In 1620, Malik Ambar reclaimed the fort from the Mughals and strengthened its defenses. Eventually, in the 18th century, the fort came under the control of the Nizam of Hyderabad and remained so until Indian independence.

C. Ausa Fort (Latur)

The Ausa Fort is a ground fort spread across 5 hectares in the southern part of Ausa town. In 1466, Mahmud Gawan was appointed as the Prime Minister of the Bahmani Sultanate, and it was during his tenure that this fort was built. Because it is situated in a low-lying area, the fort is not visible until one is very close. Some of the structures and walls show Turkish and European architectural influences.

Ausa is historically and religiously significant. During Malik Ambar's time, in 1014 AH (around 1605 CE), the town was known as Amarapur. A copperplate from the Chalukya King Vijayaditya's reign mentions Ausa as "Ucchiva Tvarishat," meaning "chief" or "superior." In the 8th century, Jain writer Jinachandra referred to Ausa as "Auchha." The famous Jain poet Kanakamar, who wrote the poem "Karakaṇḍa Charita," was a resident of Ausa, referring to it as "Asai." Over time, names like Ucchiva, Auchha, Asai, and Ausa became established. Yadava-era inscriptions mention Ausa as an administrative center. The fort spans 24 acres, 30 gunthas, and is surrounded by a moat that remains in good condition. There are several wells within the moat, and the entrance gate is named "Loha Bandi." Inside, the main gate is called "Ahashma." Within the fort are structures like the Rani Mahal, Lal Mahal, and Pani Mahal, with three notable wells known as Paribavadi, Katarabavadi, and Chand Bawdi. The fort was built during the Bahmani period under Mahmud Gawan's leadership.

Fort of Ausa

Ausa Fort held political importance historically. The city was significant since the Yadava period. In 1357, the Bahmani Sultanate established power here. Later, Burhan Nizam Shah I took control of the fort. In 1635, Mughal Emperor Shah Jahan's orders brought it under the Mughal Empire. During the Maratha War of Independence, numerous skirmishes occurred between Dhanaji Jadhav and Mughal general Zulfiqar Khan. In 1852, the British took over the area from the Nizam of Hyderabad, keeping control until 1857-58.

D. Udgir Fort (Latur)

The history of the Udgir Fort is well-documented in texts like "Tārīkh-e-Firishta" and "Tārīkh-e-Udgir." The fort was constructed between 1347 and 1527. In 1636, Mughal Emperor Shah Jahan captured the Udgir Fort. Later, on February 3, 1760, a battle took place between the Nizam and the Marathas at Udgir, with the Marathas temporarily capturing the fort. However, after the Marathas' defeat in the Third Battle of Panipat, the Nizam re-established control in the south, stabilizing rule over Udgir under the Nizam of Hyderabad.

The town of Udgir is known for Udgir Baba and the Udgir Fort. Udgir was under Mughal rule for nearly 800 years. After the Marathas captured Ahmednagar, the Nizam advanced against them, leading to a battle here on January 11, 1760. The Maratha general, Sadashivrao Bhau Peshwa, led the Marathas with Ibrahim Khan Gardi's artillery, significantly defeating the Nizam's forces. Subsequently, the Nizam Salabat Jung surrendered. Finally, on February 3, 1760, a treaty was signed by which the Nizam granted the Marathas a jagir territory with an income of 6 million, including forts like Asirgad, Daulatabad, Bijapur, and Burhanpur.

Fort of Udgir

Meanwhile, on January 10, 1760, at Buradi Ghat near Delhi, Maratha commander Dattaji Shinde was martyred while fighting Najib Khan Rohilla in the Battle of Shukratal. Afterward, Najib Khan and Ahmad Shah Abdali captured Delhi. Upon hearing this news, Sadashivrao Bhau, after defeating the Nizam, began preparing extensively and set out from Paratwada with 100,000 Maratha soldiers toward Delhi on March 14, 1760. According to the Delhi Agreement of 1752, the Marathas were responsible for protecting the Mughal Empire. Under Mahadji Shinde's leadership, the Marathas had provided protection to the Mughal Empire. Later, on January 14, 1761, a decisive battle took place at Panipat against Ahmad Shah Abdali, resulting in the Marathas' defeat.

A. Paranda Fort (Dharashiv District)

Paranda is a remarkable ground fort, known for its architecture and engineering. The fort was constructed by the Bahmani Sultanate's

Prime Minister, Mahmud Gawan, in the latter half of the 15th century. In 1599, the Mughal army defeated the Ahmadnagar Nizamshahi, but the Nizamshahi officials decided to rule in the name of the young Murtaza Nizam Shah and chose Paranda Fort, located about 80 miles southeast of Ahmadnagar, as the capital. Paranda served as the capital for a while. Between 1629 and 1632, Shahaji Maharaj took control of the fort, though it later returned to Mughal possession. Ultimately, the fort remained under the Nizam of Hyderabad until Indian independence. During the Chalukya period, Parimanda (Paranda) was an important pargana. The fort is about 35 meters in length and width. During the Bahmani reign, Mahmud Gawan built this fort. Around 1600, the Mughals captured the fort. In 1629, Shahaji Raje won the fort, but in 1632, it passed to the Bijapur Adil Shahi. The Adil Shahi general Murar transported the famous Mulukh Maidan cannon to Bijapur in 1632.

Being a ground fort, Paranda has double ramparts. The ramparts include numerous bastions. The first, north-facing entrance is grand, with battlements and arrow slits above the gateway. To the right of the entrance, three carved swans and two vyala (mythical creatures) are found on the wall. Walking within the fort, one can see stones from temples and hero stones embedded in various places along the ramparts. New wooden doors have been added to the main gate. Inside the first gate, there is a dark, arched passage leading to a second, south-facing entrance. After passing through this, one reaches a heavily fortified area surrounded on all sides by bastions with small cannons aimed at potential intruders. This area, called "Ranmandal" (war arena), is a killing zone where invaders reaching this point would be vulnerable to attack from all sides. Stairs lead up to the watchtowers above the first and second gates. Climbing up, one can see remnants of hero stones along the ramparts. Beyond this, a third, east-facing gate leads to a large bastion. Circling around it, one can walk along the path between the double walls. Guard stations are seen along the walls, and temple carvings are visible on the inner walls.

Strong Ground Fort - Paranda

The fourth gate is nearly 40 feet high, and the adjacent bastions are around 60 feet tall. A Persian inscription is found on the gate. Directly in front of the gate is a 50-foot-deep well, with a massive bastion and a cannon about 20 feet long on top. Entering through the fourth gate leads to a fifth, west-facing gate. A stunning bronze cannon, known as "Malik-e-Maidan," rests on the bastion beside the fourth gate. This 20-foot-long cannon bears five inscriptions in Persian, including one on its muzzle. The rear of the cannon is designed with petal-like patterns, and two small lion sculptures adorn it, though one was cut and stolen. The drum tower (Nagarkhana) is located above the fourth gate.

B. Naldurg Fort (Dharashiv District)

The history of Naldurg Fort is tied to the local legend of King Nal and Queen Damayanti. Initially, the fort was under the control of the Chalukyas of Kalyani. Later, it fell under the Bahmani Sultanate.

Following the dissolution of the Bahmani Sultanate, it was taken over by the Adil Shahi of Bijapur. Mughal Emperor Aurangzeb later captured Naldurg, adding it to the Mughal Empire.

Naldurg - Largest Ground Fort of Maharashtra

Control of the fort eventually passed to the Nizam of Hyderabad. Located in Dharashiv (Osmanabad) district, Naldurg Fort is a unique and ancient heritage site. It is considered one of the largest ground forts in Maharashtra, with an impenetrable fortification spanning approximately 3 kilometers, featuring 114 bastions. This fort holds a special place among Maharashtra's hill forts and sea forts. Naldurg Fort is declared a protected monument by the Archaeological Department.

Canons placed at Naldurg Fort

Hindu temples within the fort, including the beautiful Ganpati Mahal and Laxmi Mahal, are noteworthy. The nearby Nar-Mada waterfall adds to the fort's charm. This grandeur of Naldurg Fort is an invaluable part of Maharashtra's cultural heritage.

Nar-mada (Male - female) Waterfall at Naldurga

4.4 Summary

Maharashtra is home to a vast number of forts, unparalleled in quantity in comparison to other regions of India. Marathwada, in particular, is known for its historically significant forts, especially ground forts or bhuikot. While robust forts like Paranda, Kile-Ark, and Dharur are renowned, Naldurg, the largest bhuikot or ground fort in Maharashtra, stands as a key symbol of Marathwada's architectural heritage.

4.5 Self-Study Questions

Question 1: Write brief answers

1. What is ground fort?
2. How many ground forts are there in Marathwada?
3. Name any five ground forts from Marathwada

4.6 Suggested Reading/Links

1. Forts of Maharashtra
2. Saad Marathwadyatil Killyanchi - Pandurang Patankar
3. Durg Darshan- G. N. Dandekar
4. Durgavidhana - Milind Paradkar
5. Killa-Marathi Vishwakosh
6. http://trekshitiz.com

Total No. of Printed Pages: 2

SUBJECT CODE NO: - IKS-8805
FACULTY OF HUMANITIES
IKS (ALL FACULTY) (NEP) F.Y SEM I
Examination November / December 2024
Forts of Marathwada (IKS-1)

[Time:1:00 Hours]   [Max. Marks:30]

Please check whether you have got the right question paper.

N. B: 1) All questions are compulsory.
    2) Use blue or black pen only
    3) Use pencil for diagrams.
    4) Use of any signs attracting attentions is prohibited.

    १) सर्व प्रश्न सोडविणे आवश्यक आहे.

    २) फक्त निळ्या किंवा काळ्या पेनचाच वापर करावा.

    ३) आकृत्यांसाठी पेन्सिलचा वापर करावा.

    ४) कोणतीही लक्षवेधक व सांकेतिक करण्यास प्रतिबंध आहे.

Part A/ भाग अ

Q1 Answer multiple choice questions (Attempt all)   10

    1) On which fort the Charminar minarate situated.
       a) Paranda   b) Devgiri   c) Kandhar   d) None of the above
       चांद मिनार हि वास्तू कोणत्या किल्ल्यावर आहे.

       अ) परांडा ब) देवगिरी क) कंधार ड) यापैकी नाही

    2) In which dynasty Kandhar fort was built
       a) Chalukya b) Maratha period c) Rashtrakuta d) Nizam
       कोणत्या राजवटीच्या काळात कंधार किल्ल्याची निर्मिती झाली.
       अ) चालूक्य ब) मराठा काळ क) राष्ट्रकुट ड) निझाम

    3) In which district Antur Fort is located.
       a) Chh. Sambhaji Nagar b) Dharashiv c) Beed d) Jalna
       अंतूर किल्ला कोणत्या जिल्ह्यात आहे.
       अ) छ. संभाजीनगर ब) धाराशिव क) बीड ड)जालना

    4) Which Fort was situated on the Bank of Bori river
       a) Antur b) Dharashiv c) Naldurg d) Kandhar
       बोरी नदी काठी कोणता किल्ला वसला आहे.
       अ) अंतूर ब) धाराशिव क) नळदुर्ग ड) कंधार

1

University Exam Paper of November/December 2024

5) At which fort the 'Machli Tof' is located.
   a) Udgir b) Naldurg   c) Kandhar   d) Devgiri
   'मच्छली तोफ' कोणत्या किल्ल्यावर आहे.
   अ) उदगीर   ब) नळदुर्ग   क) कंधार   ड) देवगिरी

Part B/भाग ब

Q2 Answer the following questions (any four)   20
खालील प्रश्नांची उत्तरे लिहा. (कोणतेही चार)

1) Explain the types of fort in Marathwada
   मराठवाड्यातील किल्ल्यांच्या प्रकाराचे वर्णन करा.

2) Illustrate the structure of Naldurg Fort
   नळदुर्ग किल्ल्याची रचना विशद करा.

3) Explain the importance of fort in historical perspective
   किल्ल्याचे ऐतिहासिक महत्व विशद करा.

4) Analyse the structure of devgiri fort.
   देवगिरी किल्ल्याच्या रचनेचे परीक्षण विशद करा.

5) Focus on the administrative importance of paranda fort.
   परांडा किल्ल्याच्या प्रशासकीय महत्वावर प्रकाश टाका.

6) What was the contribution of yadavas in Ford development.
   किल्ल्यांच्या विकासासाठी यादवांचे योगदान काय होते?

Enter Caption

● 80 ●